Alone

By Grace Alone

An epic journey to faith

Juliana Ray

Marshalls

Acknowledgement

I wish to thank my husband for his encouragement and help that I so much needed whilst preparing my manuscript.

Marshalls
Marshall Morgan & Scott
3 Beggarwood Lane, Basingstoke, Hants, RG23 7LP, UK

First published by Marshall Pickering Communications 1985

ISBN: 0 551 011 87 4

Photo Typeset by Brian Robinson, North Marston, Bucks.

Printed in Great Britain by Anchor Brendon Ltd, Tiptree, Essex.

Dedication

'. . . and you shall remember all the way which the Lord your God has led you
make them known to your children and to your children's children . . .' To them, Shari mama's great-grandchildren, I dedicate this writing.

Contents

Page

Foreword

October 31st has always been a very precious date for us. It was Shari mama's birthday. This year, in 1972, it was her eighty-first. Because she had spent the previous one – the eightieth, the really grand occasion – abroad, we were to make up for it this time by having the immediate family together at a dinner party in our house in London.

We sat around the table thoroughly enjoying this family event. Shari mama, sitting at its head, was in great form. One story followed another with episodes from her life, some of them well known to me but new to the 'in-laws'. Her mind was a storehouse of colourful memories and her ever bubbling wit gave colour even to the sad events of the past. Then we fell silent, sharing, remembering, till one of her granddaughters-in-law suddenly turned to her and said half-jokingly, 'What you really ought to do, Shari mama, is to write down your memoirs; we will then make a book or a film of it.'

A sudden light in Shari mama's smiling blue eyes indicated that the idea pleased her. I wondered whether she wanted – or indeed would be able at her advanced age – to respond to such a challenge. It certainly caught my imagination. While the dinner party continued around me, I was miles away, in the past, already starting to piece together the mosaics of Shari mama's life, beginning with the fragments she had passed on to me about her childhood and youth. The picture which emerged was full of brightness, matching that carefree epoch.

Born in 1891 during the peaceful period of the Austro-Hungarian Empire under the rule of Franz Joseph, Shari mama was brought up in comfort and prosperity in the midst of a loving, closely knit Jewish family. Then, during World War I, clouds darkened this cosy family picture, lifting only temporarily to produce a brighter backdrop once more. From the late twenties onwards I myself was witness to and part of her life, a life in which the joy and grief, prosperity and austerity, persecution and escape, losses and new opportunities intermingled. This was the period which began between the two world wars and reached its lowest ebb during the Second World War, the holocaust and later Hungary's socialist takeover. None of the personal tragedies, material losses or immense difficulties which she endured have ever broken my mother's spirit. She faced the various circumstances with real courage, no bitterness or resentment clouded the underlying joyfulness of her nature. Then, at an age when most people start to slow down and settle for retirement, the most exciting period of her life began: she shared with us the venture of uprooting her life and settling in a new country. The transplant was completed in her final decade. Then she arrived at the peak of her life: she recognised Jesus as the Messiah of the world, accepted him as her personal Redeemer, and was born again.

To look at this white-haired, frail, little old lady, her favourite silver-framed amethyst brooch adorning the lapel of her smart light grey suit, and to listen to her witty anecdotes, nobody would connect her with the past valiant decades of European history. Yet, those faraway days were not merely the background to her life but they shaped and influenced its development. Those times never overcame her – for she was the true conqueror. It is this private life with all its joys and sorrows, unfolding within the events of nations that makes this story worth telling.

The day after the dinner party I went to buy two exercise books, one in which she could jot down memories as they occurred to her and another for writing in a more continuous fashion. So she began. She wrote much in both, mainly in note form, until she got too tired and writing became an extra strain on her. She died in 1975. I put away the notebooks and the whole idea of writing Shari mama's life story was laid aside. Too much happened in the world and in our family. The right time to sit down with a relaxed mind and recreate the past from a jigsaw of notes was long in coming.

On New Year's Eve, 1981, the same company of young people present at Shari mama's eighty-first birthday party some nine yers earlier and now with little children of their own, were reminiscing together once more. We spoke of Shari mama in particular. How sad it seemed that her great-grandchildren would have no recollection of her at all, nor of the roots out of which our family grew. Then, out of the blue, Tommy, Shari mama's oldest grandson, said to me, 'Please write down the story of our family. When the kids grow up they will be able to read about our origins, our circumstances far back in Hungary, life in years of peace and war and the conditions that finally led to our coming to England. You could write about events before your time using Shari mama's memoirs and add to them your own remembrances and experiences.'

This time I could not resist the challenge. It seemed to me more than the record of one Jewish family surviving the events of history. The story to tell was bound up with the living God acting in our lives. The clock showed one o'clock in the morning of 1 January 1982; it became a New Year resolution.

Part I

THE ROOTS

(Based on Shạri mama's memoirs)

Shari mama's family

Parents: Karoly GRABER and Irma LEIMDORFFER
Sisters: Erzsi, Manci and Lola
Brother: Pali

Her husband: Armin LEIMDORFER
his brother: Feri
his sister: Lica

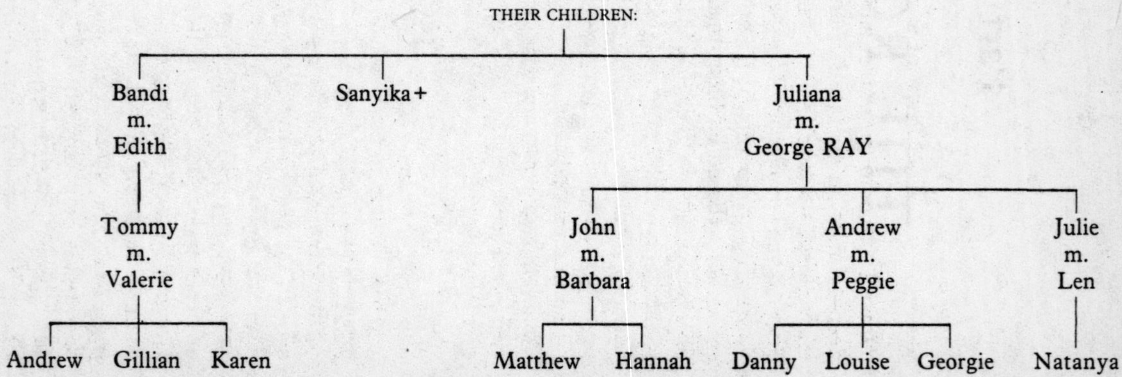

The dawn of a golden era

'When I look into my mirror and see the thousands of tiny deep wrinkles on my face I can hardly imagine that I, too, once started life as a little child.' So begins the record in Shari mama's notebook. The stunningly beautiful child in the picture in an ancient photo album was her. Yet she could hardly believe that she had once been that 'baby Shari, the beauty of Zolyom', as somebody had written next to the bouncy baby girl who sits in a kind of padded nest. The photographer had showed prophetic insight when he portrayed her in such a way: she had indeed been born and raised in a padded nest.

Shari mama's parents were very young when she was born, and were at the start of a successful life. As the firstborn she received, for a time unrivalled, all their love and care as well as the full attention of her grandparents. She seemed, in fact, to be spoiled by everyone.

When she was born in Zolyom it seemed that peace and progress had finally been established in her country, the Austro-Hungarian monarchy. This 'golden era' (golden at least to the middle and upper classes) had begun in 1867. That was the year of reconciliation. Almost two decades of oppressive rule had followed the 1848/9 revolution. Much innocent blood had been spilt in an attempt to convert Hungary from a Hapsburg vassal state into an independent country. In that year the Emperor Franz Joseph signed a peace treaty, prepared by Hungarian statesmen, which gave new rights not only to the country (now to have an autonomous government) but also to many individuals whose freedom had previously been restricted. The

Emperor's coronation as king of Hungary was imminent and there were celebrations throughout the land in anticipation of a totally new era. Now at the turn of the century there was an air of stability in the country.

Amongst other family papers there was a letter commemorating this historical event, written by Shari mama's grandfather Alexander to his young fiancée. He wrote teasingly: 'Yesterday I took part in a ball that was organised by the local Jewry (yet very elegant) to celebrate the new law that legalises mixed marriages, between Jew and Gentile. So, my beloved Annicska, I warn you, behave nicely towards me! Consider, from now on I could marry any Gentile girl I liked!.'

This excerpt shows, of course, that our family was Jewish and, although great-grandfather Alexander teased his little bride, he married her and one of their children, Irma Leimdorffer, became Shari mama's mother. From Zolyom where Shari mama was born (a small town in Upper Hungary, now Czechoslovakia) the family soon moved to Budapest, the capital. Irma Leimdorffer's husband, who was a gifted young solicitor and barrister, had his office there. Theirs was a very large household. Soon Shari mama found herself amidst two sisters (Erzsi and Manci), one brother (Pali), then another sister (Lola) and a little cousin who was brought up with them. Her father's office was part of the house and a spinster niece, who acted as his secretary, lived in too. A cook and a chambermaid looked after meals and cleanliness, while Kisa (an Hungarian nickname for 'Miss') looked after the children, keeping an eye on their general behaviour, and sewing and patching up the clothes.

Shari mama's parents were God-fearing people. But no emphasis was laid on the strict observance of any rituals or religious laws. On the greatest holy days, New Year and Yom Kippur (the Day of Atonement) they all went to the synagogue and, on Yom Kippur, they fasted. The need for the repentance of sins was a familiar concept and they understood the meaning of the prayers that dealt with it.

They also knew God was merciful and cared for them, his children, who were in turn expected to lead a life as pure and useful as was humanly possible.

Her father and mother had many friends, both amongst Jews and Gentiles; they were loved and respected by all who knew them. Her father had a very high reputation in legal circles where he was known as a defence lawyer of great integrity and skill. Even much later a mention of his name would occasion respectful remarks: 'Oh, Dr Graber is your father – he is a wonderful man.' And he was also a father much loved by his children, sensitive to the needs of the large household.

In Shari mama's words:

'Father gave us a great deal of freedom and yet there was order and discipline within the family. Each of us was made from an early age to help with some of the household duties in order to relieve mother and the servants. This was a routine which was kept with some ease – even with pleasure – because once the duty was done we could use our free time as we liked, following our own inclinations. Even on Sundays when we went out to friends, or later on when we went to dances on Saturday nights, one of us had to be home early to make the beds for the rest of the family and snacks for anyone at home so that the servants might have their free evenings too.

'One of our regular tasks, for instance, was the annual spring cleaning around Easter. At about the same time every year, my parents used to go to the Dalmatian coast (which then belonged to the Monarchy), usually to Opatija (then called Abbazia) for two weeks. This was *their* holiday – the summer vacation was for the whole family. It was our yearly "surprise" for Mamushka (this was what we called mother, whilst Daddy was Papushka) to do the spring cleaning while they were away. It was, in fact, a major operation, involving far more than just cleaning and we girls volunteered to help.

'In Hungary the summers were hot and the sunshine very

bright, hence carpets and furnishings needed protection. First, the carpets were beaten in the yard by a carpetbeater, an article few remember in this age of vacuum cleaners. Then, after a thorough brushing, they were rolled up with layers of newspaper and sprinkled with turps (the smell of this remains with me still). Then the carpets were covered with sheets of canvas, neatly tied up with string and stored away until October. The upholstered furniture was covered with special loose summer covers and the house began to look cooler. Winter coats and clothes were cleaned, brushed and tucked away in wardrobes and the aroma of mothballs and lavender was mixed with the turpentine smell; the house was now "ready" for the summer and the servants appreciated us children for having performed our share of the work.

'In those days there were very few unions in Hungary, not much protection for workers and definitely nothing for domestics, so that this "spartan" and very "socially conscious" household was quite unique and was either admired or scoffed at by those who knew us well.

'However, we children had other "musts" besides caring for the servants' welfare. There was also discipline in the sense that each member of the household had regard to all the others, especially to parents and grandparents. When one of them took a siesta, or rested because of some illness, silence was maintained as far as possible. How grateful I am even now for this lesson in adaptability and observation of other people's wellbeing. It has helped me in so many situations and has enabled me to live in peace and contentment when we have had to share our home with others.'

Childhood years

Shari mama's first home in Budapest was on the Buda side of the capital. In those days there were only two bridges across the Danube, one of them, the Suspension Bridge, having been built in the 1840s by the English engineer who earlier had built the bridge across the Thames at Marlow. Crossing the river to get to school by a boat was fun for the children. Later, however, they moved to Pest on the other side of the river and school was within walking distance from home. This school, which all the sisters attended, had not long been established; it was the very first grammar school for girls in Hungary. It was a lovely school, with excellent teachers where only the masters were formally addressed; the mistresses were called Auntie Paula, Auntie Emmy and so on. The atmosphere this created was an intimate, homely one. Great emphasis was laid in the curriculum on the arts – mainly literature – and much less on the sciences. The treasures of Hungarian, German and French literature were imparted to the young lady scholars.

Budapest is surrounded by hills, many of which are now built up, but in those days most of them were covered by forests. In the spring, when violets perfumed the still leafless woods, or in the autumn when the trees turned all shades of yellow, red and rust, the rucksacks were filled with sandwiches and the family would go hiking. This was a favourite activity for Sundays. They covered ten to fifteen miles a day, had their picnic lunch in a sunny field and then, becoming merrier as the day went by, marched along singing folk songs until dusk. They returned home tired yet refreshed by the beauty of their countryside and the unity among them. So the days went by. There was work, and there was joy. The sky of the children's young lives seemed almost cloudless.

The whole household moved every summer vacation to Rajetz Spa, to a large house that belonged to an aunt. The family gathered there for two months' holiday and it was the best time of the year. There were at least twelve children, all cousins, with their parents. Papushka was organiser in chief. He invented games for the children, took them for long hikes and initiated all sorts of competitions, like flower arranging, plant collecting and butterfly catching. There was a little mule-cart at the house. The prize for the winner of the day's competition was permission to drive the cart or ride the mule.

Such were the happy memories of Shari mama's childhood. She wrote:

'It wasn't all honey in our home, however. We had our mischiefs, quarrels and tears like any other normal children. Yet the underlying peace of our home was what mattered most and the memory of this permeates all else. As I said before my parents were very keen on freedom in our upbringing. This was continued later too, in letting us choose whichever career we wanted (a rare habit for parents in those days) and in allowing us to choose our marriage partner according to our own judgement and inclination. In all these matters Papushka's motto was: "Do, my dear, as you think best". He trusted in the good foundations which he had laid down in our childhood to produce the right fruits, healthy judgements and wise choices.

'My childhood gave me a tremendous base for the life which followed. To have such emotional, moral and financial security gave me an exceptional advantage that was to help me and hold me up in many shaky circumstances later on.'

An exciting episode

The following account is again from Shari mama's own memoirs:

'One summer my Leimdorffer grandparents invited me to join them on their holiday in Carlsbad.* I jumped at the chance: spending all my summers with my younger sisters and brother had begun to bore me – after all, I was fifteen! Carlsbad was a spa, a fashionable health resort, where middle aged and elderly people went regularly to drink the waters which were reputed to have healing properties,

*Both Carlsbad (Karlovy Vary now) and Marienbad (Marianske Lazne) belong now to Czechoslovakia.

especially for the digestive system. In my youth, well-to-do people ate much more than they do now; many were plump and had gall-bladder or stomach troubles which they then tried to cure at health spas. These spas had lovely long promenades, pavilions where bands played and benches everywhere; people walked up and down drinking the magic waters that were supposed to put right the results of gluttony. It was not the most amusing holiday for a young girl, but just because there were few of my age group around I became the centre of much attention. This, of course, pleased me no end.

'The climax of this holiday came on an excursion one coolish day to Marienbad, another spa nearby. We were peacefully walking along with many others when a wave of excitement swept over the promenaders. There was much whispering and knowing looks even between total strangers, as if there had been a conspiracy in which all the visitors to Marienbad had taken part. Of course I was most intrigued until somebody shared the secret with me too. "His Majesty the King of England and Queen Alexandra are here in Marienbad and they might even turn up on the promenade," whispered a lady into my ear, with great reverence.

"Oh, how wonderful," I exclaimed, "What if I bought a bunch of flowers and when they appear curtseyed and handed it to the Queen?"

"Oh no, beware my child," said the lady, "they are here strictly incognito and we must not embarrass them by showing any kind of recognition."

'So the great event passed by, without curtsey or flowers. For a moment I caught a glimpse of the august couple as they sat in comfortable armchairs listening to the music. The King was very elegant, almost dandyish in a sports suit, with a hat I thought very Scottish, black patent leather shoes and the then fashionable white gaiters. The Queen was very smart and regal but simply dressed in a tweed overcoat and matching skirt.

'Just like the other holidaymakers I tried to pretend they were ordinary people and that nothing special had happened on that promenade in Marienbad. Yet for me it was an episode that seemed so very exciting at the time and when I returned to school in the autumn it caused a real sensation amongst my school friends.'

Romance

Towards the end of the school year, Shari mama's mother noticed that there was a slight deformity (rather an asymmetry) about her back. One shoulder blade protruded a little more than the other. An orthopaedic surgeon was consulted and he advised a drastic gym therapy supported by various machines to at least restrain the curving tendency of her spine. He recommended that she be sent to Vienna where an excellent specialist treated such cases in his well equipped gymnasium. But how best should this be carried out? Her parents decided that they would send her to Vienna for at least six months or longer if necessary. She gladly agreed to this unexpected adventure, hoping that a stay in Vienna would consist of something more than hours of physiotherapy. Some fairly close relatives in Vienna invited her to lodge with them. All was arranged within days and Kisa rapidly equipped her with some new frocks, including one or two suitable for the theatre or even the Opera House, should she have the opportunity to be taken there.

Shari mama was never to forget that visit. She wrote:

'My mother said just a couple of days before my departure, "We cannot expect your aunt and uncle in Vienna to chaperone you all the time. You may need some younger company as well. I will visit Auntie Juli today and ask for Armin's address. We will write to him and ask him to look after you a bit while you are there."

'"Oh, not Armin, Mamushka, anyone but him! You know how he used to treat me as a stupid little kid, ignoring me altogether. He would hate to be lumbered with me," I said, dreading any such arrangement by the two mothers.

'Armin Leimdorfer was a young cousin of Mamuskha. I had not seen him for quite some time. As children he and his younger brother Feri had come, together with their older sister Lica, to family parties but, as Armin was eight years my senior, we had not really had much in common. As teenagers, Armin and Feri had had a rather notorious reputation: at every family gathering my sisters and I secretly hoped that we would be witness to some of their mischief! Kisa, who had known them from early childhood, was our main source of information and she amused us by telling us endless tales about their doings when they were very young.

'Nobody in the family believed that "those two" would ever become honest, hardworking men and everybody felt sorry for their parents. Yet, when they were eighteen and sixteen their father suddenly went bankrupt and they proved to be reliable sons in a very difficult situation. Armin started work immediately after matriculation to help maintain the family. Feri hoped to become an architect and Armin, who was not keen on college life, willingly agreed to help finance him at university.

'Then, for a year, Armin was called up for military service and during that time we hardly saw him. He continued his training in an officers' school and I met him once, at Lica's wedding, just before he left the K.u.K. (imperial and royal) army as a lieutenant. He was wearing the smart dress uniform: pale blue top and black trousers and was very good-looking. Cousin Armin at twenty-five years old had a lot of experience. He mixed with other officers, earned his own living and helped sustain his family. What could he have in common with me, a seventeen year old schoolgirl? In any case, I thought, I do not need charity and I determined not to see him at all.

'However, mother thought she knew better and, after I had been in Vienna a few days, Armin came to see me. He offered politely, though not enthusiastically, to show me round the imperial city. "You have become a pretty little young lady, Shari," he said on the way, "but I'll never forget you as the eight-day old baby I was taken to visit. All the ladies in the room outdid each other in praising your lovely features to show that you resembled this or that member of the family, but I remember being dead bored. I thought you were a screaming red bundle and nothing else." The ice broke. We laughed and became fast friends.

Armin seemed to accept the role of chaperone quite willingly and even took pride in being responsible for me. From time to time we went to the Burgtheater (the Theatre Royal) where mainly classical plays were shown ("suitable for a young girl like you," said Armin) or to the Opera House.

'It was fun to be with Armin and although his temperament was very different from mine we got on well together. I was rather placid and even-tempered while with Armin one had to be prepared for surprises. Sometimes he was on top of the world and really charming but he could also be very moody, even wilful and quite angry. I seemed to have a calming effect on him and he, in turn, brought a lot of colour and initiative into my life. I soon realised that I liked his company more and more. In short, I fell in love with him. Yet he had not shown any feelings of this kind towards me, which I found natural enough. The six months passed like a dream.

'The orthopaedic surgeon was quite satisfied with my progress and hoped he had arrested the curving process of my spine. "Your back is not healed and it will cause a deformity later, but if you keep on exercising you can delay a visible asymmetry or hump for decades," he said. So I arranged to return home.

'The last outing with Armin began as had all the others. But when the time came to say goodbye he suddenly took my hand and kissed it.

'I do not say my farewell for long because I want to return

to Budapest myself soon," he said. "I will try to find a suitable job there. And also, I have something to tell your father." He looked at me with a mischievous smile on his face. "Perhaps you will guess what that might be!" With these last words he turned and was gone. I returned to Budapest bewildered and very happy.

'I kept my secret. I reported only that Armin had taken good care of me, so that my mother was able to acknowledge triumphantly, "I told you he would help you to see a bit of Viennese life and culture. Sometimes mothers have quite good ideas too!"

'Finally, Armin turned up with a bunch of red roses for me and asked for a private word with Papushka. They disappeared into the study. "What does all this mean?" asked my mother with a justifiable frown, while my sisters Erzsi and Manci started giggling and whispering and I stood there blushing, unable to say anything. "I hope, Shari, Armin has not taken advantage of the situation when you were under his care! That would be scandalous indeed!" I tried to reassure Mamushka and praised Armin's reliability and integrity. But it had all been so sudden and surprising that she was hard to convince.

'Soon Papushka and Armin reappeared. The girls were sent out of the room and only four of us sat down to hear what Papushka had to say. "Well, my dear Irma, this is a great surprise to me and I suppose to you as well. Armin has just proposed to marry Shari. First I want to hear what she has to say. Do you love Armin, my child?"

"Yes, I do," I said.

"Well, then, I'll tell you what I think," said Papushka in his slow but firm tone. "Shari is only a schoolgirl who might easily have become infatuated by a mature young man who took her seriously; she thinks now that she really loves him. To me this is not a real basis for getting married. As for Armin, I do not doubt that his feelings are genuine. However, he has to prove himself first before I could entrust my daughter to him. I respect you, my boy, for what you have been doing for your family but you have to start in a job first, with the prospect of an established career that will enable you to keep a wife and start your own family. Therefore, I do not say 'no' to this planned union but I do not say 'yes' either. I give you six months during which you should not meet one another at all. I mean this and insist on it. No secret rendezvous. Shari – you carry on with your studies, see other young people in your free time, read, amuse yourself, and see how you feel when the time is over. You Armin, come again in six months' time, report on your job situation, and we will then talk matters through again."

'As always, Papushka's wisdom was indisputable and we agreed to his verdict.

'Soon afterwards I heard from Kisa, who always knew everything that was happening, that Armin had found a job, not too far from where we lived. One day at lunch time I happened to look out of my window and saw Armin standing on the other side of the road, just opposite our house. He looked hopefully upwards. I waved, he waved back and then went. Next day I made sure I went to my window at the same time: he was there again. And so it went on for six months! Armin passed by our house every day in his lunchtime and we had this very precious glimpse of each other.

'We kept our promise: we did not meet for six months and had no secret rendezvous. We just waved to one another – this, after all, was not included in Papushka's prohibitions!

'My days otherwise went very pleasantly during those six months. My mother made a point of seeing that I had a good time. I was invited to many parties and dances and was quite popular among the eligible young men. Many tried to court me but though I danced with them and let them visit me, none of them took Armin's place in my heart and just because I did not respond to any courtship the young men were even keener on me.

‘Time went quickly by and the six months were soon over. Armin’s visiting card came on the last day and indicated his coming on the day after. This time he must have satisfied Papushka because they came out of the study together, smiling.

“What about me? What if I’ve changed my mind?” I asked, teasingly.

“Come on,” said my mother, “you would not have stood at half past twelve every single day in your window if you did.”

“So you knew?” we asked in unison. There was a lot of laughter. I blushed, and Armin got his “yes” from everyone in the room.

‘A few days later I was due to go to a ball but this time Armin was to come as well. When my suitors queued up asking for dances I just said, “Sorry, gentlemen, all are booked for tonight.” The consternation grew when the “stranger” arrived and received all my attention. There was whispering among the mothers too. “It is not done, not proper that a girl should let herself be courted so obviously. And who is he anyway?”

‘Next day our engagement was announced in the Sunday paper. It was a surprise even to the wider family circle and of course to all our friends. That morning we walked arm in arm along the bank of the Danube on the Pest side. This was the “corso”, a promenade frequented by people especially on sunny Sundays, where they met friends. We had to stop every minute, so many people came up to us with their congratulations. In the afternoon and evening various family members from both sides of the family came to express their good wishes. How well I remember it all. There was kissing and laughing everywhere.

‘Then Papushka asked for our attention and gave a little humorous fatherly speech. At the end of it he said, “All should be well with these two and I would say it is a wonderful match; there is just one thing I am a bit concerned about: it is Armin’s clan!” and turning to

Mamushka he said sheepishly, "What do you think, my dear, will it do?" There was a minute of consternation; then the penny dropped that we were all related and roars of laughter broke out from all present Leimdorfers.

'Then Papushka said, "Let me present you, Armin my son, with the golden watch that I was given on my engagement day by my father-in-law who, incidentally, is your mother's brother." He took out of his pocket a golden watch hanging on a golden chain. A very special watch it was, and is! Grandfather Alexander Leimdorffer had received it from his employer, Baron Popper, for whom he was a "man of all seasons". In title he was the chief forester of the baronial estate but he was also the manager of the baron's finances and sometimes even a companion of the baron's son on his various travels. The back of the golden watch carried the baron's coat of arms, a green fir tree. It was of exquisite enamel work, but the main feature of the watch was its chime. When a little button was pressed it chimed the quarter hour and the minute of the actual time.

'Everybody admired the watch and while it went from hand to hand Armin called me aside. He produced a little box from his pocket that contained a lovely diamond ring which he slipped on my finger. I noticed on the box the name of a Viennese jeweller. "When did you buy this ring, Armin?" I asked.

"Just before I left Vienna, six months ago!" he said.

I laughed and accepted with joyful resignation the fact that my future husband was a very determined young man who knew exactly what he was after.'

So ends Shari mama's account of how she fell in love with my father. I could almost see the smile on her beautiful face as her aged eyes looked back.

Out of the padded nest

After their marriage the young couple went to Berlin for their honeymoon. One day Armin took Shari mama to the races and she soon discovered that this was a real passion with him. He was stimulatd by the horses. Their beauty just fascinated him. The excitement of betting was part of the passion. One day they lost a great deal of money and Shari mama began to worry about how they would manage during the rest of their stay in Berlin.

'Don't worry, my dear,' Armin said reassuringly, 'I will replace the money very soon.'

Next day they went to a casino. Armin played with great confidence but, alas, within a couple of hours, their purses were empty! Shari mama was in despair!

Luckily, they had some relations in Berlin (as they had in most central European countries) and they went to visit them. After overcoming their embarrassment, they confessed what had happened. Well, to a honeymoon couple all is forgiven! They received enough money to see them through – which they repaid afterwards in monthly instalments! After that Shari mama asked her young husband to promise never to attend horse racing and gambling casinos again! This he did and kept his word all his life.

Shari mama's new home in Budapest was a flat. It consisted of three main rooms: a lounge, a dining room and a bedroom. On arrival a young girl, whom Mamushka had employed as domestic help while they were away, appeared. 'I kiss your hand, madam and sir,' she said smilingly as she opened the front door. The new bride made a great effort to appear very grown-up and dignified, though she was, if anything, probably younger than the maid.

In July the following year (1912) Shari mama's little boy, Bandi (Andrew) arrived. The next two years of her life were fully taken up by this wonderful child who was not only beautiful, with silver blond curls, rosy cheeks and big blue eyes, but was also a sweet-tempered, easy little boy.

They adored this little chap and it was a pity Armin could only spend short times with him. By the time Armin arrived home from work it was nearly bedtime for Bandi. In those days Saturday was a full working day and even on Sundays the office was open until midday and the employees were meant to be there. Armin had a strict boss who made his staff work pretty hard.

Thus, in those 'good old days' of the middle classes, whilst the men had to work much harder than they do now, married women hardly ever went out to work. Women had a lot of leisure time to spend on reading, visiting one another, and needlework such as crochet or other embroidery to embellish their homes.

To an extent Shari mama conformed to this kind of life, but not whole-heartedly. She was not keen on spending time with other ladies gossiping or complaining about the domestics. She found it 'stupid and boring'. Yet, for a while, that became her way of life. She visited her parents at least twice a week and on Sundays they visited Armin's parents. This meant a longer journey. They went by cab, crossing the Franz Joseph bridge to Buda where Armin's parents lived. It was fun to watch other people walking across the bridge while they proceeded slowly in the long line of cabs. Some young men used to spend hours walking up and down on the bridge especially when it was a bit breezy: then the skirts of the walking ladies would occasionally whirl up in a sudden gust of wind, and their ankles would be tantalisingly revealed.

Life then seemed firm and stable, rock solid with its daily routines. Prospects for young couples were good. They could look forward to having more children, because the means to keep up a growing family and a bigger home were financially assured for those who were prepared to work hard. Their world appeared unshakeable.

The shaking of the unshakeable

The summer of 1914 was exceptionally beautiful. Shari mama spent a month at Lake Balaton with Bandi. Armin managed to get his Sunday mornings off and came down every Saturday evening by train and stayed until Sunday night. Bandi played for hours building sandcastles in the sun, becoming so tanned that the contrast with his light curly locks made him even more attractive.

Like an explosion into this idyllic existence came the news of the assassination in Sarajevo of the Crown Prince and his wife. Immediately came the ultimatum to Serbia. Then one event succeeded another with bewildering speed. Before we could grasp what had happened, the army was mobilized. Armin had to report to his regiment. Shari mama rushed home with Bandi to Budapest and within days had to say goodbye to Armin whose regiment was commanded to leave. 'It won't be long,' he assured Shari mama.

On the station platform stood many wives, mothers and sweethearts who had come to see their loved ones off. The train was packed with soldiers and horses, and decorated with flowers and flags as if it carried a wedding party. The young soldiers sang and waved as the train moved off, and kisses were blown to them from the platform. Neither they nor those who were left behind suspected that many of them would never return. None of them guessed that their world, so solid just weeks before, was on the brink of a major catastrophe. It was to shatter an era of peace, and the world was never to be the same again. The First World War had begun.

The following months were spent eagerly reading the daily news in the hope of seeing the end of the war soon. They hoped in vain. Instead, the war became more and more widespread, involving more and more countries. Gradually, the post that had brought comforting letters of reassurance delivered telegrams containing a few words of condolence and praise for the heroism of the young man who had been sacrificed to the 'Fatherland'. The postman, at first hailed with so much joy, turned into the most dreaded figure. The panic lasted each day until delivery time and then started again the following morning.

This was how Shari mama lived as well. Then, she had a surprise. Her notes read:

'One morning just before Christmas, the bell rang. I rushed trembling to the door. "Good heavens! Armin – is that you?" This sounded a very stupid outcry but then the soldier in the doorway was so unlike the elegant officer who had left a few months before. The creased, dirty uniform, the long hair and gingery beard had transformed Armin into someone almost unrecognizable. He evaded my embrace, warning me of possible insects in his clothes. I rushed him into the bathroom where he stripped, bathed and changed. Then he went to see his son. But Bandi screamed at this stranger with the ginger beard. Reluctantly, he returned to the bathroom and shaved off his beard to please his little boy, but left his accustomed black moustache.

'Later our domestic girl went to the bathroom to clean and wash Armin's clothes. Seconds later she burst into the living room: "Madam, the bathroom is swarming!" We rushed about with disinfectants, the underwear was burnt and the uniform bagged up and sent to a de-licing station. I was shocked.

'"How did this happen to you?" I asked with compassion.

"My dear, all of us were full of them. There was no sanitation, no means of washing in the trenches."

'This was as much as I succeeded in pumping out of Armin. No details, no stories about the war were ever brought up in conversation during his short leave. He carefully avoided the topic. I realized then that he was deeply affected by the horrors of the war and wanted to forget about them, at least for a little while.

'All too soon he had to go back. This time the train carried no flags, no flowers. The young men were joyful no more. Dreams had been shattered as the realities of the war had hit home to everyone, soldiers and civilians alike. At the platform Armin did not say "it will be all over soon". With a kiss he just turned quickly away saying, "Try to take care of yourself and Bandi, and God be with you." This parting was even worse than the first. But it was the fate of all the women on the platform, and the common fate, the common sorrow, made it seem easier to bear.'

For a while Armin's letters arrived regularly. Then they ceased. No letters came but, thank God, no telegram either. This at least was reassuring. Finally, the long awaited letter arrived from Armin, written from a hospital. He had caught some kind of illness in the trenches that had affected his lungs; it was not TB, he emphasized, but it needed treatment. Despite his illness it was, of course, a tremendous relief for Shari mama to know he was alive and in good hands.

The war years and after

A few weeks after hearing about Armin's illness, Shari mama received a letter from him. He was much better but before resuming his military duty he had been sent to a convalescent home for officers in Meran (now Merano) in the South Tyrol, and she could join him there, with Bandi. Of course she went; indeed, she could not prepare quickly enough for this unexpected journey.

In the early spring Meran was a paradise, a peaceful haven. The best hotel had been allocated to convalescing officers, and they lived there like princes, as if the war did not exist at all.

As before, Armin did not speak much of his wartime experiences; he avoided the topic in the same way as he had on his leave. Yet, one day a notification came from his regiment that Armin had been recommended for distinction because of his bold, brave and excellent behaviour. But he just shrugged his shoulders. He was neither happy nor proud with this news.

Finally, the doctors' verdict came: Armin was fit for duty again, but only behind the front line. No more trenches and all the dangers of the war front! This was fantastic news for which they were very grateful. From then onwards Armin was always stationed at some fairly safe place and for the rest of the war years Shari mama and Bandi were able to go everywhere with him. Some kind of family life returned and soon their second little son, Sanyika was born.

When Armin's distinction was confirmed and his silver medal arrived, it was pinned on him at a little ceremony where it was also announced that he had been promoted to first lieutenant. Shari mama asked him afterwards what exactly he had done to merit this double honour. She was never to forget his answer: 'Look, my dear, I carried out as best I could the command I was given. That was all. To tell the truth I hate the memory of the hand-to-hand battles we fought with other young men like ourselves whom we had no reason to hate. They were fighting us only because they, too, were commanded to do so. You see, I do not consider either honour or glory to be part of this war. It has no moral justification at all. It is nothing but butchery.'

With this short conversation the subject of Armin's 'heroism' and honours was closed for ever. The silver medal, which fascinated Bandi, was sometimes given to him to play with when he was a good boy, otherwise it was put in the glass cabinet amongst the other ornaments. Little did they suspect that at a much later date it would have a significance in their lives.

They had enjoyed a temporary ease, but early in 1918 there came a new horror that shook everyone: the epidemic of 'Spanish flu'. The death toll was stunning; victims disappeared from their military circle. Shari mama lived in fear that her children, so close to the sources of infection, might catch the disease and she did her best to sterilise and disinfect her home.

In the autumn of 1918 the war finally came to an end. Whatever its cost, the joy of peace was indescribable. Armin got his leave and they returned to Budapest to resume city life.

It was wonderful to see their family again who on their part were delighted to meet Shari mama's little boys. Bandi was now six, ready to start school, Sanyika was two and as beautiful as a little girl with his coppery-blond curls.

While Shari and Armin were away new in-laws had been added to the family at home and little children to the young couples. It was fun to meet them all. But what caused them the greatest joy was that Manci had married Feri, Armin's brother. The two sisters had become sisters-in-law, a situation they constantly found hilarious!

It was not easy to pick up the threads of normal life after a break of four years. Armin's pre-war job was no longer in existence. But with the help of a loan he managed to purchase a sizeable quantity of timber in the Southern part of Hungary and found a way to transport it by barge on the Danube up to Budapest where he sold it. This was his first independent transaction and this was how he launched his own firm. The building trade, held back during the four years of war, was now reviving and Armin's small firm was established in relatively favourable conditions. In fact they were all very conscious of how privileged they were and how mercifully God had kept them without loss of life. This was much to be thankful for! Hardly any family had been spared some grief; many women wore black, mourning the loss of loved ones.

The autumn of 1918 left little time to brood over the past. The moderate start to the revolution, begun by left-wing social-democratic intellectuals, soon took a more violent turn. The leaders and the Communist red guards stirred up the feelings of the poor and oppressed. There were many such who, after the devastation of the war, had become desperate and had nothing. In 1919 the revolutionary government introduced drastic and sudden changes which affected everybody. Middle-class people lost their jobs and many professions came to a standstill. Lawyers, solicitors and barristers stopped functioning as the red government took over the courts of justice. Papushka and many of his colleagues met daily on the steps that led down from the Houses of Parliament to the Danube. There they sat in the sunshine, joking, never losing their sense of humour and hoping that the revolution would not last too long. 'People will wake up from the intoxication of sudden power and will realize that they need all sections of society to pull together to help the country rise out of economic disaster,' they kept on saying to one another. However, inflation and considerably reduced income took its toll. Food supplies became very scarce. Long queues appeared at bakers and butchers where women stood half the day to bring home a meagre supply of food.

In the summer of 1919 Shari mama, Armin and the two children spent a few weeks, for the children's sake, in a cottage on one of the hills near Budapest. The shops were quite a few minutes walking distance from where they lived and sometimes Bandi and Sanyika went to the baker in the morning, to queue up for bread. They loved to bring home the fresh hot loaf and could hardly wait for Shari to cut them a piece each. One morning they went as usual, but took simply ages to return. Shari mama, feeling very worried, went to meet them. About halfway down the sloping road she found them, sitting in a bush munching the fresh bread with great delight!

'They were so sweet when I found them, Bandi and little Sanyika, looking up at me with big blue eyes,' wrote Shari mama. 'The sight of the two of them in the bush on that bright summer morning has stayed so vividly in my mind, the memory of it so sweet and yet so painful. My little boys, my darling little boys!'

Her memory of 1919 was a painful one indeed. In the

next chapter I have left Shari mama to tell her story herself.

Grief within – grief around

Shari mama's notebook continues:

'Sanyika suddenly ran a very high temperature. We sent for the doctor who seemed quite concerned. The night was endless. We sat next to his bed and tried to cool his little body. By the morning his temperature suddenly and drastically dropped. We were quite relieved but when the doctor returned he seemed even more worried, called Armin to the other room and prepared him for the worst. A few hours later it was all over, our little Sanyika had gone. A later version of the Spanish flu had caused his death. What we felt and how grief stricken we were I cannot express and do not want to describe. Only those with such an experience could possibly understand how terrible is the loss of a child.

'For a while I felt like a robot. I performed all my duties, kept our house clean, looked after Armin and Bandi, but inside me there was utter despair. My little Sanyika had left a huge emptiness in my heart, which it seemed nothing could ever fill. Of course, I had met grief before. In the past I had felt compassion for mothers who had lost their little children, or their sons in the war. To be sorry for people is one thing, but to identify with their grief is quite another. This I believe is only possible after personal experience.

'Once I had recovered from that initial agony I was able to recognize this truth. I came to accept the loss of my child as an experience which would enable me to enter into deeper understanding of other mourners.

'Then, many many years afterwards I read the 53rd chapter of Isaiah. The 'Suffering Servant' carried all bitterness and sin on his own shoulders. He was a man 'acquainted with grief'. I remembered my own suffering and my realization of the value of it. An echo in my heart cried, "It is true, it is true, there was no other way – not even for God!"

While Shari mama was preoccupied with her personal grief the world around seemed to be reflecting her darkness and despair. The dictatorship of the communist revolution of 1919 was short lived. During this time there were many atrocities committed which embittered the middle and upper classes. After the fall of the communists in the autumn of 1919 the revenge was terrible. The right-wing, so-called 'white' anti-revolutionary forces (in contrast to the 'red' revolutionaries) ruthlessly carried out executions without proper trials. Many of the victims of this 'white terror' were wrongfully accused and antisemitism flared up because many Jews had taken part in the communist revolution. What truth there was in this was widely exaggerated, and the facts were deliberately distorted.

In 1920, Miklos Horthy, the last Admiral of the Austro-Hungarian monarchy, became Regent of Hungary. He tried to restore law and order to the land. But can a path lead to general restoration when the wayside is strewn with gallows? Can righteousness and peace grow out of injustice and personal revenge? Any hopes for a new beginning were undermined by the peace treaties of 1920 which the victorious Allies forced on the countries that lost the war. Hungary was deprived of about two thirds of her former territories and population, a large part of her industry and almost all her raw materials. The economic situation was grave, with inflation gathering momentum. Many businesses were bankrupted and many people ruined.

Even then, things could have improved, given some honest soul-searching and a willingness to seek out a truly democratic framework of government. But neither individuals nor state had learned from the past. For some the good old days seemed, on the surface, to have come back. They were the ones who had not gone broke in the twenties and whose background had not been 'spoiled' by revolutionary activities. Once the overhanging sword had lifted slightly, people, fools that they were, forgot that it could fall again. Those who still had the means to do so carried on with their lives as before, as if nothing had happened.

This is how it was with Shari mama and her family. She wrote:

'I am writing this with the benefit of hindsight, with present knowledge. It is by no means the criticism of an outsider. I, and the whole of my family were amongst those fortunate enough to start again and soon prospered.'

Armin's business expanded and they lived under the 'great illusion' that all would be well again in due course. Only in later years did they realize how blind they had all been. Shari mama wrote:

'It never occurred to us that more was expected than honest labour, a proper family life and donations to charity, after which your free time and your money were there to be enjoyed.

'Then in 1923 our little daughter Juliana – or Juci as we called her – was born and this new baby finally healed our personal wounds, too. Happy times, laughter and amusements returned until the sword above our heads was lowered once more in the thirties. It was by God's grace indeed that our family was aware of its descent. We saw the writing on the wall before many others had begun to realize the danger. We noticed a change of attitude. Long before we ourselves were affected our attention was drawn to people who had been stricken. Our involvement with their fate prepared and fortified us for the events that lay in store for us.'

These were the last sentences of Shari mama's notes. I now take up the thread of the story.

Part II

AXE ON THE ROOTS

Interlude

It was the 12 March 1938, the night of the annual Timber Ball, an event attended by everyone connected with the timber trade. For my parents it was a real 'must' as my father was the president of the Timber Federation. I will never forget that night, it was to become so significant for us and for the whole world.

I was in my teens and the social events of my parents and my brother Bandi were a matter of excitement and also of envy on my side. There were still a few years to wait before I would be part of such glamorous occasions! For the time being I had to be satisfied with observing their preparations for outings like this ball.

My father just finished his second shave of the day; he and Bandi – who by then worked in my father's timber business – both wore their dinner jackets, with stiffly starched white shirts. I thought they were so elegant, so handsome!

Finally, Shari mama appeared from her bedroom, beautifully yet discreetly made up, wearing her new evening clothes. The style she chose was so much in tune with her character that I exclaimed spontaneously, 'Mummy, you look smashing!' Over a very tight black skirt she wore a little black velvet top that was like a lady's version of a dinner jacket. She wore a soft white blouse, interwoven with fine golden threads, which together with her wavy blonde hair, contrasted beautifully with the plain outfit. She looked chic and charming.

'Oh, if I could only go with you,' I sighed, not comforted by the fact that on such 'left behind' occasions extra goodies were prepared for my supper.

Suddenly, the telephone rang. It was Uncle Feri who asked whether they had heard the evening news on the radio.

'What? They just marched in? Incredible!' Pale and agitated, my father told us the news. The German army had marched into Austria and annexed it to Germany. It was the day of the 'Anschluss' – tragic for millions.

All the joy and excitement that had been in the air before the telephone call died in a second. A foreboding clutched at their hearts which I could not help seeing, though I did not fully grasp its significance.

'Let's stay at home,' Shari mama suggested, but on second thoughts this was dismissed.

'I can't be absent,' said my father, 'after all, as the president of the Timber Federation it would not go unnoticed that I had abstained; this would cause an even worse panic.'

With grave faces they went, as if they were going to a funeral and not to a ball. Little did I know that this was to be the last ball they would ever attend, and that my dream to be taken to such an occasion was gone for ever.

The 'Anschluss' was life's turning point for millions of people. After the first panic on the memorable night of the Timber Ball important changes came about in the pattern of my family's way of life. But let me first come back to my childhood with Shari mama.

* * * * *

Memories of my childhood with Shari mama

Before that fateful evening of 12 March 1938 my childhood had been happy and largely carefree.

My abiding memory of Shari mama is of somebody who sang to me a lot. She had a lovely soft voice and the tunes she sang were light and easy to remember: melodies from operettas by Strauss, Lehar and Kalman as well as from original folksongs.

The charleston mania hit Hungary as it hit elsewhere. I remember our first gramophone, with its big horn sticking out. It was kept in our lounge and often, late at night when I was supposed to be asleep, I heard faint music, so one night I sneaked out and peeped through the keyhole of the lounge. I was stunned by what I saw. The furniture was heaped into the middle, the carpet was rolled up and my mother and father together with their friends – ladies and gentlemen whom I respected and whom I considered very old and dignified – were jumping around at the edges of the room. Their feet were twisting like those of puppets to the sound of some wild music blaring from the gramophone. 'Aha, I am supposed to respect these grown-ups yet when they think us children out of sight this is how they carry on!' I was indignant indeed.

Next day, when my big brother Bandi came home from school, I asked him whether he knew what was going on in the lounge. He just shrugged his shoulders and said that grown-ups must have their amusement too!

Shari mama had an inexhaustible fund of stories, some fairy tales and some real episodes from her own childhood. I used to have my evening meal earlier than my parents and at bedtime Shari mama would read to me, usually from a Hungarian or German book. She used to read about half a chapter leaving off at the most fascinating point. This was meant to encourage me to finish it for myself, which I did because I was so interested in the outcome. My father usually returned from his club during this reading time and brought me a bar of chocolate which I munched while reading the last pages.

Because Bandi was eleven years older than I, and an independent teenager, it was like being an only child. I loved the company of other children. Playing with my cousins, Gyuri, Nushi, Marika, Hedi, Marci and Marti, was always an extra treat. Sometimes we played at my father's timber yard, where his office was also situated. This was a big site at the side of a main railway station. The timber shipments arrived at a normal-gauge siding but a narrow track ran within the yard for internal transportation. When a part of this track was not in use we sat on the waggonettes and rolled ourselves to and fro along the site. What super fun it was!

In the middle of the site was the big shed with the sawmill. I can still hear the shrill noise of the saws and remember the smell of sawdust in my nostrils. It was all so exciting. Around the office building there was a small flower garden. This was Shari mama's work and delight. In one corner we had a sandpit and when we got tired of the fun in the timber yard we built a sandcastle, carrying water in little buckets and basking in the hot sun.

My greatest treat, however, was to visit Auntie Manci and Uncle Feri, where I sometimes stayed for a few days. Uncle Feri had designed their house, which the whole family referred to as the villa. It was built on a hillside opposite the station for the cogwheel railway that went up the Buda mountains. It was a lovely house with a huge terrace and a very big garden full of flowers and trees that were wonderful to climb. Manci and Feri had no children and could therefore spend a lot of energy and money on other things. They were like second parents to Bandi and me but were equally affectionate to the other children in the family.

Every Sunday afternoon a 'family day' was held in rotation in the various homes. We children played in the nursery but were also allowed to join the grown-ups for a while, when we wanted. Those were delightful times, with fantastic teas consisting of savouries and, above all, delicious cakes, each household competing to produce something better than the week before. Although the cakes were actually prepared by their respective cooks, it was the housewives who took all the glory!

I vividly remember the atmosphere of those family days. Grandpapushka used to tell juicy stories of his various court cases or express his opinion on something while all present listened respectfully. He was the natural head of the larger family, although a humble and unassuming man. The respect which he attracted was not just 'good manners': he was loved and cherished by children and in-laws alike.

There was lively discussion too, mainly among the men, about politics or the economic situation, while the ladies sat in another corner, knitting or crocheting. That is, all the ladies except Shari mama. She was always in the midst of the conversation or discussion; ladies' chatter was not for her. She was far more interested in serious topics and I noticed that when she gave her opinion the men present listened attentively. 'Sure, my mother is the brightest of the ladies,' I thought.

One day we had exciting news. Grandmother phoned to tell us that Grandpapushka had been given an honorary title by the Regent, in appreciation of his services to the courts of justice. (This was equivalent to a CBE.) He was to have an audience at which he would thank the Regent in person. The title meant that he would, in future, be addressed in some untranslatable way (something like Honourable Sir) and the servants happily made immediate use of this. However, they and some waiters in the Barristers' Chamber were alone in using the title. Grandfather preferred to keep quiet about it. We, though, were very proud to have such a special Grandpa.

Guests in the home

Our house was a very hospitable one where we received many people. By the time I was allowed to mingle among the guests the charleston craze was over and there were other kinds of parties which usually ended with games of bridge at several small tables. First, of course, there would be the buffet table, laden with delicious goodies. The ladies arrived in smart evening gowns and the men in black ties. They chatted and ate, and again Shari mama, apart from being an excellent hostess, was always in the group of men, listening to and participating in their conversation.

My favourite guests were Auntie Manci and Uncle Feri. They came at any time, just dropping in when they felt like it. They would phone some time during the day and say they would be coming over that night and bringing their supper along with them. I am sure it was not only the fascination of the different food they always brought along that made their visits so attractive to me. These two were simply my favourites, perhaps because I felt how close they were to Shari mama and my father alike.

I remember a few evenings in the 1930s when many people were invited, not only close friends. I learnt that these gatherings were for the special purpose of fund-raising. A certain gentleman came to speak of a land that used to belong, and would again belong, to the Jews. At the moment this place consisted mainly of desert land that had to be purchased from its present landowners and transformed for habitation. Trees would have to be planted and houses built for those who already lived there. Who were these people? Some had been persecuted in Russia and some were enthusiasts who believed in the building of this new land and had left their comfortable homes in order to become pioneers in Israel. They called themselves Zionists, this man said. Our guests listened and were persuaded that this was a deserving cause and donated big sums towards it.

I remember many things I heard and saw in my childhood – because I was given the opportunity to listen and to take them in. In those days children were not permitted to talk at the table unless spoken to. This way I learned a lot involuntarily, whilst sitting and listening at the dinner table or on the occasions when I was permitted to mix with the grown-ups. Thus, I have my own early memories of the years of the 'great illusion', as Shari mama called them. But soon, even for me, the illusion began to fade.

My first disconcerting experience

For several years we went to the same resort on Lake Balaton. We rented a big villa with some others in our family and moved down with our entire households. It was not like Rajetz had been in Shari mama's youth, yet we children enjoyed ourselves almost as much as she had done. The villa was very near the shore and a wooden jetty led down to the water: at its end was a small platform where we sunbathed. It had steps but we could also jump into the water. In the afternoons we went to play in the little forest, scented by the needles of the Mediterranean pine which covered the ground like a thick, soft carpet.

Idyllic as it sounds now, in some sense it was very different from Shari mama's own childhood. For the poison of antisemitism had crept into the air. It had started in the twenties and become more obvious in the thirties, even before Nazism had become prevalent in Germany. The illusion created by equality before the law was misleading.

My first taste of this poison occurred at this peaceful summer resort, Balatonföldvár. There was a yacht club and a tennis club for holidaymakers, yet my parents and Bandi always played at hired public courts and never attended the yacht club. Once I asked Shari mama why this was and she tried to explain the situation to me: 'My dear, we do not go to these clubs because we are not wanted there.' This was absurd to me; so far I had always been wanted wherever I went, and by everybody.

'And why is that, please tell me; are we not good enough to be club members?' I asked.

'No, Juci, they think we aren't because we are Jewish,' she said.

'But surely there is nothing wrong with that?' I persisted.

'No, certainly not. We have different beliefs, that's all. But the members of the club do not like Jews; they are prejudiced against us.'

'What is prejudice, Shari mama?'

'Well, it is a bit difficult to explain but I'll try. Some people dislike others not because they know them personally and find fault with them, but because they are in some way different. Then they don't want to mix with them, they despise them and believe them to be inferior to themselves.'

'Oh, such people are really nasty,' was my verdict.

'Not necessarily or not wholly,' explained Shari mama. 'You see, they might have been brought up with these ideas or have heard them from their parents or at school, or they might have got them from newspapers and then adapted the ideas to their own situation. Otherwise, they might be quite nice people.'

'Tell me, Shari mama, do you yourself have such prejudices against people?'

'I hope I haven't. At least not that I know of. And I can assure you, if I ever discover such a thing in me I will try with all my strength to overcome it and stamp it out.'

Sometimes I passed by the tennis club or the yacht club and stopped at the fence to look in, curious to see what kind of people were those who didn't like us. True, I thought, they don't seem to be nasty at all; nice young ladies and young men, having fun and obviously feeling very much at home with one another. For the first time in my life I felt an outsider, someone who did not 'belong'.

Later on at school and during the persecution it was rubbed in much more forcefully; yet decades later, whenever this 'not belonging' feeling returned, it was Balatonföldvár and the clubs there that I associated with it. From deep within me the painful memory of the little girl would emerge, standing at the fence and peeping wistfully in but remaining on the outside.

On religious and school matters

My father's family was more religious than Shari mama's so she adapted herself to him and a few more traditions were observed. Apart from the big holy days, New Year and Yom Kippur, we went occasionally, albeit not regularly, to the synagogue on Friday nights. We also celebrated the Passover night when many of the family gathered around a big table and the significance of the different dishes on the table was explained, together with the reason for commemorating the occasion. There was always a big silver tumbler on the table on those Passover nights, with wine for the Messiah who, according to what I was told, might arrive at any time.

Bandi, as a teenager and as a young man, was faithful to his prayers. I noticed that sometimes when I burst into his room in the early morning he had a curious tasselled white shawl around his shoulders, a little hat on his head and some funny black straps around his fingers as well as a little black box fixed on his forehead. I was amazed to see all this and wondered why. He told me, he needed these objects to pray with and he tried to explain their symbolism to me. I did not understand why men had to pray like this whilst each night I said my little prayer together with Shari mama just as I was, in my nightie, putting my hands together. Well, this was one of the many mysteries that puzzled me then and many were added to it in later years.

Basically, I knew that all my family believed in God. So

did I, as much as a child could comprehend God in a liberal Jewish home. At school I loved religious instruction. I was fascinated by many of the Bible stories but disliked all the compulsory Hebrew reading. I found it stupid to be made to read a text parrot-fashion without understanding it and even to recite it by heart. I was sometimes puzzled about what the other children learnt, those of other religions, when they went into their respective classes for Religious Instruction. If what they were learning was also true, why didn't we learn the same things? Why did we all have different beliefs? And if what they were being taught was untrue they must be misled. And yet, from the glimpses I had had of the Catholic priest or of the two kind-looking ladies teaching the Calvinist and Lutheran children, they certainly did not look in any way less respectable than our rabbi.

These were additional mysteries I sometimes pondered, mainly at Christmas time when all the other children, the Christians, prepared excitedly for their holiday and decorated the Christmas trees we did not have in our home. But at about the same time we lit our Chanukkah candles to celebrate another miracle that was very different from the one 'they' told me about. For a little schoolgirl it was difficult to find out where the truth lay.

When our dear Grandpapushka died in 1936 I faced for the first time the reality of death and the experience of a funeral. I was frightened and bewildered since the loss was great, even to me. I have never forgotten, to the present day, the loving attention I always received from Grandpapushka or the beautiful stories he invented and told us grandchildren. For eight days after the funeral, Grandmamushka, Shari mama, her sisters and her brother sat mourning on low stools as was the custom in Jewish homes after a bereavement, whilst people came to express their sympathy. Food was brought in by friends and relatives so that the immediate mourners could just sit and remember and occasionally cry. It was all very, very sad. The ladies wore black for a whole year and only during the last two or three months put a touch of white on their outfits according to the strict tradition of the time.

When it came to my secondary education, at the age of ten, the obvious choice was provided by the 'Veres Pálné' grammar school, the very same school that my mother and her sisters had attended. I remember the day of my enrolment about a year before I was due to start.

We were seen into the deputy headmistress' office where a grey-haired old lady sat and looked sternly through her spectacles. 'Oh, it is you Aunt Paula,' Shari mama exclaimed with sudden recognition, 'I kiss your hand,' (this was how children greeted adults or men the ladies) and at the same time she did something that I found most amusing. She made a polite little gesture with her feet, a smaller version of the curtsey I was meant to make on meeting my grandparents. It was an automatic reflex from her school days.

The deputy headmistress was puzzled for a moment, obviously searching her memory for a face and a name, 'Ah, Shari Graber, of course it is you, my dear; and this is your little daughter whom you bring to us. Very well, I hope she will be as good and pleasant a student as you were.'

After being thus introduced, the grammar school held no terrors for me and I was looking forward to the day when I would begin attendance. When I actually met the other teachers I found one more mistress and one master who had taught my mother and they were especially kind to me, occasionally referring to me as 'my little granddaughter.' It was nice to see how my mother was respected, even after so many years. However, I was expected to follow in her footsteps and excel in what I did. As at turned out I was all right: I learned well, was among the top four in my class and retained this position right through school. (But I was never the first!)

The first wind of Nazism

After a couple of years in the grammar school, spent in the delightful atmosphere which I have already described, things began to change. The change began slowly but then gathered momentum. It was something like an extension of the yacht club problem I had encountered in Balatonföldvár, but gradually it spread into many more aspects of life.

Shari mama warned me several times that I would have to be very well behaved at school and learn even more diligently than before. 'You see, my dear, we Jews are more and more disliked because of some nasty propaganda that has been spread against us in Germany. Now it is beginning here too. But we will try to prove that it is untrue. We will prove this by our extra good behaviour, extra decency and determination.' Thus, even at this early stage, a common responsibility was being made very clear to me and I understood it well.

Very gradually even at school one could detect a difference in the atmosphere. No more 'Auntie Paula', now we had to address the mistresses as something like 'Lady Teacher'. When we went down in the morning to the head with the register, we had to present ourselves in a very formal, rather military manner. In these and many other details a new kind of discipline, almost a military rule, was introduced. Even our uniform was changed. Earlier we had had to wear sailors' blouses of the usual, internationally known design. These were now out and in came blouses that looked almost like hussar tops, with cravats and hats too, very Hungarian in style. All this emphasized the patriotic line.

Bandi also came home with some really alarming news from the university where he was studying for a law degree. In 1930 he had passed his matriculation with the best possible result and had then gone abroad to Switzerland to do a two-year diploma course in commerce. After this he had enrolled in an Hungarian university as an extra-mural student, only attending occasional lectures and taking the exams. At the same time he worked in my father's firm which was now quite large. According to him, student 'Jew-bashing' had become a regular occurrence, in fact it was a 'dare' carried out by the Nazi sympathisers.

'But what did these Jewish students do?' I asked. How did they provoke such dreadful insults?'

'Just by being Jewish; that alone is now becoming a crime,' said Bandi sadly. 'Even though the percentage of Jews has been greatly reduced by the so-called "numerus clausus", they still do not want to tolerate the few who remain.'

'What is "numerus clausus"?' I asked.

'It means closed numbers; in this case, the number of Jewish entries to higher education,' he explained. 'Even if they have excellent school reports?' I asked amazed. 'Even among those, they only select a few, a very few,' said Bandi.

'But who makes these rules so unfairly?'

'It is our government, under the influence of the Nazi regime in power in Germany.'

'But then our government is unfair too!' and with this conclusion my belief in the authorities was shattered.

In 1936 or 37 we went on holiday to Austria and there, for the first time, made the acquaintance of a real Nazi family. They were staying in our hotel with their teenage children with whom I made friends. Whenever they met another car with a swastika flag or sticker they joyfully raised their arms in salute with a loud 'Heil Hitler'. We had long conversations with them and were amazed to see how genuinely enthusiastic they were. When I told them that we were Jewish they said: 'Well, that doesn't matter, you may be different from the others; but the Führer is right in all things so what he says about the Jews must be true.' Here all arguments had to end. Yet this family was neither nasty nor in any way monstrous, just a family like any other – well-to-do, well educated but totally blinded by the dynamic personality of Adolf Hitler and his masterly propaganda.

I was fourteen in 1937. Ours was a very strange existence in those days. On the one hand our normal family life and my father's business life continued as before but, on the other hand, events in the outside world, although not yet affecting us personally, were touching relatives and friends abroad and the danger seemed to be steadily growing for us too.

Changes in life patterns

After the German attack on Austria in 1938 important changes came about in the pattern of my parents' lives and in the lives of other members of the family. As Shari mama said in her memoirs, they perceived the dangers of the future and faced up to them well before others did.

With the benefit of hindsight one may say that what was coming was obvious. Yet surprisingly most Hungarian Jews hoped that they would be spared the fate of the German and Austrian Jews. They believed things would never come to such a state in Hungary, that they would be safe. Most of those not personally affected lived as if the sword was not hanging above their heads too.

Although we were not yet financially affected, both my parents and Aunt Manci and Uncle Feri decided to give up their present homes. With times changing rapidly, Jews might soon be expected to live more modestly. The lovely 'villa' was sold and our spacious and comfortable apartment too. This was a voluntary move and I do not know of anyone else who had so anticipated the signs of the times. The new accommodation was comfortable but on a much smaller scale.

The two sisters, Shari mama and Manci, decided to finish with their superficial social life. The bridge parties came to an end, the balls and dances too. They offered themselves to a charity organization instead and did voluntary work in the afternoons. (In the mornings, Shari mama still worked in my father's office and Manci worked as a commercial artist.) Shari mama, coming back from the slum areas where she visited the needy, kept on telling us stories of a kind of poverty we would never have believed existed. She made friends with every family in her care, taking their worries to heart and was determined to help them. She had a special way of caring, most unusual for her time. In those days Shari mama's contemporaries would appear on the scene, administer gifts of charity and then go home feeling satisfied that they had done their good deed. In their wealthy surroundings the unfortunate were soon forgotten.

Shari mama and Manci approached their charity work differently. Insofar as was possible they identified themselves with those in need, trying to lift them out of their situation by sending at least one member on a training course that would enable him or her to earn a proper living. Instead of doling out charity they bought tools or a simple machine that would ensure a profitable occupation. They also found temporary homes for children whose parents were in particular difficulties in districts regarded as slum areas. I often heard about all this. Yet instead of feelng compassion for these people, I often felt sorry for myself. It seemed to me that I was nearing the age when I had hoped to be embarking upon a life of gaiety, of theatre-going, fashionable gowns and ballroom dancing. I felt deprived. All I heard day in and day out were stories of misery, poverty and horrific tales of concentration camps built in Germany and Austria for the Jews of those countries. Writing today, now I know how great a privilege it is to have been involved, at least in some measure, in those tragedies. Now I can thank God that it was all useful preparation for times to come.

But my dear Shari mama knew that a young girl needed some outside interests, and while she devoted herself to her poor I was given the opportunity to enjoy literature, music and art. I was bought a season ticket to the Opera House and went there every fortnight, together with my cousin Nushi. Shari mama also realized that learning to dance was necessary for the upbringing of a young girl. The time might come when all this misery would be over and I would need the skill. She looked around for something more professional than my brother Bandi's occasional instruction. She contacted some other friendly mothers and organized a course for teenage boys and girls. It was strictly exclusive and was held in a school of dancing, hired by our group once a week. There the dancing instructor did his best to transform us, clumsy teenagers, into graceful ladies and gentlemen. Meanwhile, the girls' mothers sat around the edges of the room greatly amused by the progress of their offspring.

I was past fourteen at the time, my skin covered with teenage pimples and my eyes often adorned with red styes. Big mouth that I was at home, my confidence deserted me amongst the boys. I had therefore to face the fact that unless the dancing master sent a boy to dance with me I was hardly ever asked.

Shari mama made no comment but found a good way to help me. A big Christmas party was prepared for those on the course. For this evening Shari mama wrote a long poem about Father Christmas peeping through the window of the dancing school to see what was going on. The poem made fun of the dancing master, the clumsy boys and the girls whose mothers gave them secret signs about their deportment, encouraging them to smile and so on. It was a very funny poem and she made me learn it by heart; she even taught me how to recite it.

At last the party was on; nothing was announced beforehand and it was a surprise when I stood in the middle of the dance floor and entertained the company with Shari mama's masterpiece. My success was enormous; there were roars of laughter all over the place. Then, when the music restarted after the break, I could not believe my eyes. Three boys rushed at once to ask me to dance and for the rest of the evening I was in great demand.

Shari mama sat with a contented smile. I think she believed that she had launched me on to a path of quite unforeseeable successes which might greatly influence my later life.

1938: An eventful year

In the summer of 1938 my parents sent me to Switzerland to learn French and there, on 1 August, 1938, I had one of the most memorable experiences I have ever had. The first day of August is a Swiss national holiday. It commemorates the liberation of that country from a cruel dictatorship. It is a story that has always had a special significance for me – Swiss freedom was something so wonderful, so different from the prevailing atmosphere in Hungary, that even with my childlike mind I felt exhilarated by it. On this particular day we climbed a hill so that later on we would be able to see the lights that were lit on the mountaintops and take part in the local festivities. However, I left the party before dusk for a little walk. Soon I was quite alone, sitting in a field that sloped down into a deep valley. In the grass around me thousands of different wild flowers gave colour to the late hour of sunset. Gradually the sky turned violet on the horizon and dusk crept over me. There was absolute stillness, no sound, no breeze, and then from down below the faint sound of cowbells reached me as the animals headed for home. For the first time in my life I felt God's presence and knew that he was real. Suddenly, I wanted to know more about him and I decided to go to the synagogue more often when I got home again.

At around the close of our stay I received a sad letter from home: Grandmamushka had suddenly passed away during a heart attack. I cried a lot after receiving this news.

Like the outward journey, the homeward journey from Switzerland had to be made through Italy instead of the much shorter route through Austria because, since there were Jews in the party, no visas could be granted through Nazi-occupied territory. I never thought that that journey in 1938 would be the last abroad until 1957, nineteen years later, when we left Hungary for good. Between these two dates we lived as if in a state of internment during which we did not know whether a death sentence or liberation was waiting for us at the end.

My parents were at the station to meet me. Shari mama was all in black, yet she seemed comforted, or perhaps she concealed her feelings to cheer me up. A new car was waiting in front of the station – a surprise. 'And there is yet another surprise for you that we have kept secret: Bandi is engaged,' they said.

'Is it Edith?' I asked with excitement. Of course it was her.

Edith was very pretty; her skin was as velvety as a rose petal and she had very light blue eyes and a kind of purity radiating from her. This was not only due to her fresh perfume or to the good soap she used, or to her spotless and always immaculate clothes, there was purity in her whole being, innocence combined with sophistication.

'And when will the wedding be?' I asked.

'They are planning to get married in December.' It was sensational news.

In the autumn of 1938 a Viennese uncle arrived from Dachau, the concentration camp where Austrian Jews were detailed. Prior to the German occupation, Uncle Max had been the managing director of the biggest insurance company in Austria. Now he came to us a broken, trembling old man. He had received permission to leave the camp on condition that he went abroad immediately. It was then that the reality of Nazism, of all of us becoming its victims, drew closer.

Uncle Max said only a few things about his camp life and never in my presence. As long as it was legally possible he stayed in Hungary but in 1943 he had to emigrate still further and went to Israel.

In December, Edith and Bandi got married, as planned. It was an odd wedding party. The ladies were still in mourning for my grandmother and to be in line with them, Edith also wore a black dress and a black hat with just a few violets adorning it. I was bridesmaid in a black velvet dress with a lovely cream lace collar and I carried a bunch of pink carnations, the only bright colour present. I had received the flowers from Edith's brother, Bundy. Twelve years my senior, he was a smart young man with a little black moustache and dark hair. His dream was to go abroad and buy an island where he would take all his and our family to live in peace away from all the wickedness of the world.

'And I really mean this, Jucko,' he would say to me, 'and I hope one day my dream will come true. Then I'll return and take you all with me.'

Soon after the wedding he left to take part in a tennis championship in England and instead of coming back after the tournament he stayed on. When the war broke out he joined the British army. All contact was then lost with him until the war was over.

Edith's family were very sweet people, more religious than any of us and Edith was raised to be a faithful Jewess. My parents grew very fond of her and she became a true daughter to them.

Parallel tracks

I was in the sixth form of the grammar school, still two years from matriculation, when I began to dislike school life more and more. My dislike was keeping in line with the increasing political slant to the subjects we were taught. Then a very dear form mistress of mine was suddenly and prematurely made to retire. We all knew the reason: her liberal anti-Nazi views. This, for me, was the last straw. Attendance at college was by then almost impossible for Jews anyway, so I decided to finish with school at the end of the year.

As I had promised myself, I went more frequently to synagogue during this last school year. The preaching was sometimes good, at other times rather mediocre and my pursuit of God was not too successful. His presence was simply a feeling I had from time to time, but intellectually I was still unable to find answers to many disturbing questions.

At one of our Religious Instruction lessons we were required to read aloud from the Hebrew text, the same text that had already plagued me in primary school. At this lesson I burst out shouting and crying: 'What is all this reading for, when we don't understand it anyway? Why don't you, sir, tell us about God? Where is he? Why does he allow injustice and discrimination and even persecution if he loves us? Why are we Jews called the chosen people, what are we chosen for? To be insulted, degraded by all other people? Is this how God loves us?'

It all ended in sobs and the poor rabbi, who was, anyway, incapable of dealing with an emotional teenager, could give no answers to my tormenting questions.

However, just because these questions had tormented me so much and because I could find no satisfactory answers, I had discarded the whole topic from my mind. Life was full enough of practical problems to solve. Why complicate it with abstract speculation?

For me the immediate problem at that time was to decide what to do and what to learn after leaving school. My father had the possibility of emigration vaguely in mind and thought it would be best if I learned sewing, dressmaking and fashion designing, a trade that is useful everywhere in the world.

The Salon Rosenthal was in the best part of the inner shopping centre of the city. We went one day to have a talk with the owner who, apart from running the establishment, travelled twice a year to Paris to buy model gowns there. It was a big fashion house with two main departments, one for ladies' dresses and another for coats and two-pieces (where the tailors were mainly men). I was introduced to the chief designer, a lady called Margit, who ruled an army of workers like a queen. She was excellent at her trade but was a real bully whom all feared.

Normally, girls served three years of apprenticeship, attending evening classes as well, before they took their professional exam. However, in view of my higher school qualification I would be able to take this same exam in eighteen months' time. This meant that I had to be given special treatment in order to learn the trade faster. For this extra treatment my parents paid a substantial tuition fee to the owner of the place. Margit disliked this arrangement utterly, as I found out soon after I started work there. She made a point of treating me exactly as she did the other apprentices. Consequently I was used to fetch sandwiches for the staff from the adjoining shops and even glasses of beer for the menfolk, just as the other girls did. On the way, big glasses in my hand, I sometimes met some of my mother's friends or my aunts who happened to be shopping in the area and were horrified to see me in my white overalls, doing such menial tasks.

'Never mind, my dear, you should not be ashamed of doing an honest job, whatever it is – it will do you no harm whatsoever; your crown will not slip off your head if your humble activities are witnessed by others,' was Shari mama's usual comment and she made me laugh about it and even to be proud of this situation.

My life was now running on double tracks or, in fact, treble tracks. During the day I worked as an apprentice. In the evenings I attended language courses, went to concerts and read a lot to make up for the missing years of my school education. I was also invited to friends and, apart from the apprenticeship, lived like any girl of a well-to-do middle class family.

Then there was the third track: the political situation was turning from bad to worse for us. War broke out between the German Third Reich and the allied West European countries. Hungary, being in the camp of the Berlin-Rome axis, was prepared to get involved as and when told to do so.

Laws and regulations restricting the employment of Jews affected thousands of families. To Shari mama's families in the slum areas were added many Jewish people who could no longer pay their rent in better districts and had to move out to join the poorest of the poor. Many Jewish ladies began to learn some trade, even those whose husbands were still running their own businesses or were otherwise not yet financially affected. My aunt Lola, for example, decided to train as a pastry cook: if things got worse she hoped to earn a living instead of her husband who was still the director of a large company but expected to be sacked any day.

Shari mama's life was also running on various tracks, even more so than mine. Paradoxically, in the tightening political situation my father's business was expanding with the leasehold buying of forests in territories recently returned to Hungary. Wood came to the timberyard mainly from these sources. That my father was in a position to carry on his business unhindered was due mainly to the fact that he had been an officer in the 1914–18 war, had been decorated for outstanding bravery and had received the silver medal, the one he had never boasted about and rather despised. Jews with such extra honours were at first given extra rights though later on any such privilege was withdrawn.

With the expansion of business Shari mama's secretarial duties in my father's firm had also grown. Her social work increased daily as the need for a helping hand spread into wider and wider circles. She was also greatly concerned about Bandi, who was now called up for longer and longer periods yet who, as a Jew, had been stripped of all previously acquired rank and was exposed to rude insults from any sergeant-major who happened to be anti-semitically inclined. Then parcels had to be sent to some of our Austrian relations who had not been as lucky as Uncle Max and were kept in concentration camps with hardly any food supplies. (The gas chambers had not yet been introduced in 1940; Jews in the camps were used for work nobody else was prepared to carry out.)

During this eventful period I met George, who started to call me regularly on the phone and visited me several times. He was seven years my senior, had a good job, was an intelligent young man from a good family background and so our growing friendship was approved by my parents. On my seventeenth birthday, among my other presents, there was a bunch of red carnations from him.

All went well until one moonlit summer night beckoned us on to the roof terrace of the house where we lived. We admired the illuminated city beneath us and George put his arm around my shoulder, gently. So we stood, silently yet totally absorbed in one another, not hearing the light steps of Shari mama approaching. Only when she was right behind us and said something casual did we realize her presence.

Alas, too late! When George left and I went to bed Shari mama came to sit at my bedside. 'My dear, I would like a word about the little intimacy I happened to witness today, if you don't mind.'

'But Shari mama, it was nothing but a friendy gesture by George,' I protested.

'Well, this is how all flirtations start. It soon leads to more intimacy and finally you might even have kissed!'

I was not too horrified by this prospect, yet according to my mother this was something only engaged couples should permit themselves. 'Otherwise,' she said, 'a young girl might kiss several boys before deciding to marry and thus not keep herself really pure for the one that will become her husband.' Then she added, reassuringly, 'Never in my life have I seen a young man who gave up a girl because she was not permissive enough; on the contrary, the more reserved a girl is the more the man seeks after her.' Her advice sounded wise to me and I kept it . . . for a while.

Bandi and Edith were very sympathetic to my friendship

with George and took us out several times in the rowing boat. George was a good oarsman and the four of us went on day-long excursions. I remember one Whit Sunday morning sitting in the boat; the men had stopped rowing and we were enjoying the perfect silence of the calm river. We were far from any town and could only see a village a little way away and the steeple of its church. Bells began to ring in the distance, calling people to prayer. What was it that it reminded me of? Just as years ago on the Swiss mountaintop I had heard the cowbells from below, I now experienced the same sensation: a kind of presence, the loving, all-embracing presence of God.

That was our last outing together with Bandi and Edith.

Happy events under darkening clouds

Bandi was called up again to march with the army into one of the newly regained territories in Transylvania, now re-annexed to Hungary by the 'generous' Germans. They had done the same thing to a part of Upper Hungary somewhat earlier and this was how they had ensured the gratitude of the Hungarian government and the sympathy of the people. The cost of regaining these areas was to be great and bloody but many who thought they were good patriots rejoiced in the rectification of the 'injustice' done to the country by the treaty of Trianon.

George was also called up several times for duty in forced labour camps introduced especially for Jewish young men who for some reason had no military training. (Jewish by origin that is, irrespective of observed religion.)

So came the winter of 1941. This time Bandi's division got their marching orders in the direction of Russia. We made a quick farewell on the platform, waving and crying—and he was gone. Edith was just beginning her pregnancy and we all hoped that by the time the baby arrived Bandi would be with us again.

Bandi's letters came fairly regularly and this was reassuring. In spring 1942 George proposed to me and we considered becoming engaged. However, there were problems to overcome. One was that I wanted to postpone wedding preparations until Bandi was home again. Also, George, Jewish in origin, was by religion a Roman Catholic; his mother (divorced from his father) having decided to change their religion when he was still a young boy. They were christened without any conviction, which they never had for Judaism either. They were not the only ones who made such formal 'conversion'. Many families, hoping to escape the repeated waves of antisemitism, thought to do so by putting their religion down like an unwanted garment and choosing another that seemed more suitable. We had many friends who joined one or another of the Christian churches. Some never attended any services afterwards nor did they receive any serious tuition; some, on the other hand, became interested and even professed that they believed in the teaching of their new religion. Our family greatly despised such a cowardly step taken to save one's skin. 'They behave like rats escaping from a sinking ship,' my parents used to say. They did not break with those friends but they condemned their action and so did I. And now here I was with a husband-to-be who was one of these 'feeble characters'!

When I talked over this problem with George he promised to become a Jew again as soon as the war was over since there was not much chance of embarking on such a complicated procedure right then. As far as Bandi's absence was concerned, we would leave the decision of the timing of the wedding to our parents. The night came when George intended to ask for my hand. We sat around at supper together after which the 'talk' was supposed to take place. Suddenly the bell went. The maid opened the door and came to announce that a couple wanted to see my father; they spoke German but did not say who they were. Father went to the hall and we heard voices, quite a lengthy conversation, then my father returned and we heard them go.

'Who were they?' Shari mama asked.

'I really don't know,' my father shrugged, but we could see he was most agitated. 'A couple who claimed to be relatives of mine but I have never heard their name. Liese something, like Telemann, she said, and Arthur, her husband. They came illegally to this country, so they said, and wanted to take refuge in our house. They say they come from Slovakia where Jews are taken into camps and then to a place called Auschwitz to be gassed and burned there.'

'But this cannot be true!' Shari mama exclaimed. 'Maybe they were agents – provocateurs sent by the secret police to find a reason to arrest us if we let them hide in our house.'

'I thought that too,' said my father, 'what they said could not possibly be true.' I was very upset, not just because the mood for George's proposal was gone, but because I was very concerned for the couple. 'And what if it was the truth?' I asked. 'Where will they spend the night?'

'Well, I gave them some money and an hotel address, so don't worry, they won't be in the street,' said my father and we finished the meal in silence. It took a couple of hours to recapture the right atmosphere for bringing up the topic of our marriage, but finally, that night, made so memorable by the sad episode, I became betrothed.

Next morning at breakfast my father suddenly stopped eating. 'Good heavens! Now I remember that a second cousin of mine once removed was called Liese and she married a man whose name I never knew. Oh, the little fool, if only she had mentioned her maiden name! You know, Shari, who she is, Alfred's niece. How can I find them and help them? And if it is true what they said – but can it be? Gaschambers, burning?' He rushed to the telephone and rang the hotel to which he had sent them. 'Thank God, they were still there. They are coming here instantly,' said father with great relief. Thus we escaped from an unforgivable deed: barring our home to those in real need.

They soon arrived and it was established immediately

that they were indeed the ones my father thought they were. Afterwards they often visited us for meals and my father covered their hotel expenses until it was arranged for them to go to Israel. Luckily, the authorities never found out that they had spent all that time illegally in Hungary. Our country at that time was still a refuge for Jews escaping from abroad and their stories confirmed what Liese and her husband had told us. So we lived in the expectation of the same fate – and in the hope that somehow it would never happen to us.

At our engagement party I met all George's relations, his divorced parents, uncles and aunts, his two young cousins and the head of their family, the grandmother whom all respected and feared. On this occasion George was presented with the pocket watch with the crest of Baron Popper; according to family tradition it was now to become his.

Concerning our wedding arrangements, my parents themselves suggested that we shouldn't wait until Bandi returned. Times were too uncertain, in fact our very lives were too uncertain, so we should get married whilst weddings were still possible at all. We decided on October but the date was brought forward when the air raids started and George's call-up for the labour camp was once again expected any day.

Our wedding was simple and modest; even so, looking back, I admire the way my parents were able to put aside their permanent anguish for Bandi and rejoice with us in our happiness. Bandi himself wrote a very loving letter, without betraying sorrow that he had to be absent from this family occasion. Because of the difference in our religions, our wedding took place in a registry office, followed by a family lunch in an hotel. From there we left to spend our honeymoon in a holiday flat on a nearby hillside. It was not glamorous but we needed to be on call in case George had to answer any urgent summons to the camp. Indeed, it came after six days. We rushed home quickly and packed his rucksack.

So George was gone too and I moved back to my parents' place as if I had not been married at all. My flat, newly bought and furnished, with all my lovely trousseau and gorgeous wedding presents, was deserted. I visited it sometimes and hoped that one day we might be allowed to live there.

Birth, accident and new beginnings

In October 1942 Tommy was born to Edith and Bandi. He was a lovely baby and most of our attention was now focused on this little newcomer. He was the first of the new generation since there had been no children in the family for a long time. Many photos were taken of him and sent to Bandi, who yearned for his little son and counted the days until he could see him in person. However, instead of this hope becoming a reality, his letters ceased after January 1943. The siege of Stalingrad was on and we knew he was in that area. Some other wives of men in his battalion, with whom Edith had come to be close friends, had the same experience: no letters arrived any more.

In the midst of this anguish Tommy's exceptional sweetness captured our hearts and greatly comforted not only Edith but all of us. Shari mama carried on with all her work and so did my father, yet every evening they went to be a while with the baby. Shari mama often tried to cheer Edith up by telling her of her own experience when my father was away in the war and how one day the post had brought the letter that made all well. Surely this would happen again. But time dragged on and no news reached us from anyone belonging to that battalion. Then we heard through the BBC (to which we listened nightly in order to hear reliable world news) that thousands and thousands of Germans and other troops has been captured and taken to central areas of Russia as prisoners of war. We now hoped that this had been the fate of Bandi's division and that once the war was over they would be able to come home again. It was a meagre hope but it kept us going.

In March 1943, six months after our wedding, during which time George had hardly been home for more than a few days at a time, I was visiting a friend in a nearby small town when I received an urgent telephone call. It was Shari mama: I should hurry back to Budapest at once and go straight to a military hospital because George had had an accident and had been taken there by ambulance. She tried to break the news as gently as she could but at the end she said, 'Do hurry, my dear.' (Only later did I learn that the telephone message she had received said that if his wife wanted to see him alive she should hurry. Poor Shari mama had to bear the brunt of the shock, I was spared the worst of it.)

What had happened was that George's labour camp group had been working on a building site and while he was up on some scaffolding it had collapsed and he had fallen from about the second floor on to his back, where he lay unconscious on the ground. He had been taken by ambulance to the hospital and was apparently still unconscious when my parents had arrived there. When I reached him he was able to smile faintly at me and to say, 'It will be OK.' He had regained consciousness just minutes before I arrived. He was in agony day and night for two weeks afterwards, yet apart from a daily inspection no nurse came into the room where the Jewish boys were kept. They were separated from the other patients. The young men helped each other with bedpans and so on as best they could. George was not alone in his bed either; as a rule, two shared a bed, each of the four beds in the room being allocated to Jewish 'labour campers'. Only when the X-rays showed that George had broken two vertebrae was he given a bed on his own. Even in the X-ray department he overheard the radiologist (a brother of one of the most notorious Hungarian Nazis) saying, 'Now that's enough, we won't take any more pictures of this case, a Jew isn't worth the films that are so costly nowadays.'

No treatment followed those X-rays for some two weeks. This was more than my father could bear. Could he accept that his son-in-law should suffer ill-treatment and no medical help in this military hospital? Did he have to stand by without being able to help? After a while he found a way: an investigation revealed the name of the consultant who visited the hospital's orthopaedic cases. He went to see this surgeon privately and offered him a considerable sum of money. Together they plotted how this doctor might, by 'mere coincidence', enter the Jewish room, which was out of bounds for him, and find a case that was interesting for the sake of his 'research' and then ask for permission to treat it.

It happened according to plan. The snag was that by then the vertebrae had started to grow together in the wrong way. Before setting the spine in plaster they had to be rebroken and stretched into the correct position. This was done by suspending George by his hands and feet, causing the spine to curve and the wrongly grown pieces to break, and forcing them back into their correct positions by the sheer weight of his body. Several times he fainted from the pain, which was not eased by anaesthetics. Finally the operation was completed and he was encased in plaster from his neck to his hip bone. With this plaster he became mobile, no longer bedridden.

How he stood up to all this suffering and humiliation I never understood; there were no complaints, just encouragement for me that all would be well. Altogether he was in that hospital for six months. With his plaster on he was able to help the other bedridden patients and also to keep the hospital rule which decreed that he should carry his own bedframe once a week down to the hospital yard where it was deloused. This involved burning through the iron frame and mesh to kill the bedbugs hidden inside. Yes – bedbugs were everywhere, on the wall, under his plaster, biting no end. The only relief came to him from scratching himself with long knitting needles. According to George, this was the most irritating thing he had to endure!

One day while all this was going on, an extraordinary person visited our home. This was not to be just a chance encounter, it was to have the greatest significance not only to my life but to others too. This is what happened.

The firm that had supplied my furniture sent along a woman whom they said was a specialist in making the loose covers which I needed for protecting the upholstery in summertime (as was customary in Hungary). She was Polish, but we were able to converse in German. While she was busily cutting the material she started chatting. 'You are Jewish, I believe?' I was taken aback by this directness. 'You have a lovely flat,' she commented and then carried on, 'a great collection of books too; do you have a Bible?' This I found even more bizarre. After all, religious matters are private. This woman was a bit too inquisitive I thought.

'No, as a matter of fact I have none,' I answered, wishing to put an end to the conversation.

Yet she carried on, 'Do you at least have an Old Testament that you read and know?'

'No,' I admitted, becoming somewhat embarrassed.

'Oh, isn't it sad,' she commented, with real sincerity in her voice, 'a daughter of Zion and yet she does not know her own scriptures.'

Daughter of Zion? What an odd but lovely way to describe a Jewess. I have never heard this expression before. She continued with a few more pertinent questions, then she put down her work and started to tell me about herself.

She was a Gentile girl who had married a Jew in Poland; at present she was sharing the fate of her Jewish husband and had come as a refugee with him after Hitler's occupation of Poland. From her story I realized that her predicament was worse than mine, yet she radiated peace and joy. When I questioned her about the source of her optimism she spoke of the love and care of God for mankind and for each of us, his children. This sounded absurd to me.

God, loving mankind? God, loving me personally? I could not see much sign of it!

She explained that cruelty, persecution and war are the consequences of sin that men individually commit against God and against one another. God gave us all free will: it is his most precious gift. When we use it for evil instead of good we cannot return the responsibility to God for the outcome. But God has not discarded us, he still loves us and is with us in all our griefs and sufferings, in all the tragedies of men.

I still could not see what comfort this could be and asked, 'What proof do you have that what you say is true?'

Then, for the first time in my life, I was presented with the good news, the Gospel, as a reality. The lady spoke about Jesus as the expected Messiah. He came to teach us how to live a human life, as God had intended in the first place and he not only taught, he lived according to his word. He himself tasted disappointment, difficulty and endured hatred, yet had overcome them. His was a redemptive life in the sense that he came as a servant to all mankind, a Suffering Servant, who carried all the sin, sorrow and sickness of the world on his shoulders. With his sacrificial life and death he opened the way towards 'restoration' for every individual who hears God's calling and wants to live according to his will.

'But where are these "restored" people?' I asked. 'I've not met many so far, if at all. And how can you believe that the Messiah has already visited this earth when what we see around us bears no resemblance to the circumstances characteristic of that golden age? According to the prophets there will be peace and joy on earth, spears transformed into ploughs and even nature will be transformed, wild animals will become tame!' I retorted, using the little biblical knowledge I still remembered from my childhood.

'Now, think this out for yourself,' the lady said very gently. 'Can such ideal messianic conditions exist while the individual man is selfish, corrupt and wicked? Does not man have to change first to be able to enjoy such perfect conditions and to maintain them? Doesn't the transformation of the individual have to come first and the new conditions afterwards, as its consequence? But be sure that God is working towards this end and despite the detours caused by man's disobedience the messianic age will dawn on us. It might not even be far distant. Jesus will return to this earth and with him all those who have been 'restored' over the centuries. With them he will govern and heal mankind and even nature will be transformed.'

'You said Jesus will return, but where is he now? And what is he doing? Just observing our present misery from a distance?' I asked. 'No,' said the lady, 'Jesus is not an observer. When he was resurrected from the dead he returned to his Father and has been representing mankind in Heaven ever since. He is pleading for us corporately and individually as someone who understands our needs, because he went through it all himself. His present role is that of a high priest but when he returns he will be our king—and every knee shall bow to him.'

I was more and more amazed as she spoke. She presented these matters with such authority that I was convinced she not only believed them but *knew.*

'But why not search for the truth yourself?' she added. 'You don't have to accept what I tell you, start to read the Bible, the Old and the New Testament and think about what you read and judge for yourself.'

She finished her work and left me with a friendly smile. I have never seen her again. Her name was Mrs Schaffer. Most likely she disappeared in one of the concentration camps (or gas chambers) where Jews were taken when they were deported from Hungary by the German Nazis.

I would have forgotten this episode in all the turmoil of our life then but it was meant to be otherwise. For some time I had planned to take English lessons; a good friend of mine had recommended an English teacher but had warned me that 'she is one of those believers'. That aroused my curiosity and I met Mary Hajos. Soon I met her husband Emil too, originally an orthodox Jew but now a Christian, who knew both the Old and the New Testament well. They invited me to attend Bible studies held both in their home and in a Lutheran church. I became more and more interested but was unable to take for granted everything I heard. I argued, debated and questioned everything but, following their advice, started to read the Bible and interpret it for myself. In the end it was neither Mary nor her husband, but the written word that convinced me. I read all the Gospels first, looked up references to the Old Testament, read the prophecies and finally came to the point when I had to ask myself: was Jesus, of whom the Gospels draw such a perfect yet realistic portrait, a dreamer, a madman or a false prophet? If he was none of these, then I must believe that what he said of himself was the truth. And didn't one prophet after another foretell, and describe, a Messiah like him? Isn't Isaiah 53 a perfect description of Jesus and his ministry on earth?

Eventually, I began to feel sure of my convictions. Of course I would have loved to share them with George but there was hardly any opportunity for this while he was in hospital because we were never alone there. However, at last the day came when, still encased in plaster, he was permitted to leave the hospital temporarily. For the very first time we could move into our little flat. His accident had been in March, 1943 and it was now November.

When we had settled down I brought up the subject, carefully and cautiously, knowing that George was something of an agnostic and religious matters were outside his interest.

However, I found him more pliant than I had anticipated. 'I confess,' he said, 'that during many sleepless nights I often asked myself what life was all about and why there was so much suffering and injustice in this world. Is there a God at all? If so, does he care for mankind, or do things happen without any preconceived order or plan, haphazardly and unpredictably? Then I considered my own case. I could just as easily have died or become a permanent cripple. Why had I been granted more time to live? Was there something I had to learn? Had I a purpose to work out?'

When he shared these thoughts with me I ventured further and asked him to come along to a Bible study with me. He was hesitant. 'I'll tell you what, my dear, I'll come with you once, for your sake and to show that I am not altogether antagonistic to what you now seem to believe. However, if I find that this philosophy is not to my way of thinking, promise me that you won't insist on my attendance in future; it would be a waste of time anyway.' I promised and we agreed.

An occasion arose quite soon. It was not unprepared: Mary and Emil, who only knew George from my account of him, prayed that the Holy Ghost might touch him at the first encounter. And so it was. Not that he said much about his impressions. It's not his style. But he came again next time, without comment.

A few relatively settled weeks followed; George's plaster was removed and a steel corset replaced it during the day. He resumed work in his office in the hope that he would be able to continue there, since he was war disabled and therefore unlikely to be sacked or called to do any more forced labour. Although the price had been high in terms of pain and suffering, under the circumstances his accident might have turned out to be a blessing in disguise.

Christmas 1943 arrived and for the first time it was *our* Christmas. George and I went to buy a little tree, decorated it and on Christmas Eve sat in candlelight and sang together some of the hymns we had learned, feeling a real affinity with other Christians throughout the world who were all celebrating the same thing at the same time.

In January 1944 I came to a decision: I wanted to be baptized. I felt that I wanted to bear witness publicly to what I believed. I wanted to belong to the 'body of Christ', to join the ranks of true believers. I believed that in the

Church there was a place for both Jew and Gentile and that the barrier between them should be broken down and also that if I wanted to enter into this united body I would have to commit myself to it. I knew it would not change my Jewish identity, neither in myself nor from the point of view of recent legislation, which was based on racial rather than religious discrimination.

Mary and Emil arranged the little ceremony in a Lutheran church and we combined the occasion with a blessing on our marriage, so far legalized by the civil authority only. It was a simple yet moving service; first, my christening, then the wedding vows and the consecration of our marriage. Only Mary and Emil, Shari mama and Ilonka mama (George's mother), were present, the two dear mothers, who were unable to share our spiritual experience, yet would not have missed an occasion so precious for their children.

The reaction to our 'conversion' was very mixed in the family. The greatest opponent was Edith who was shocked by it and we had many discussions, that led nowhere, of course. My parents accepted that we had chosen a different path; whatever they may have felt, they certainly never expressed bitterness or resentment. The heritage of Grandpapushka the great democrat, whose principle was to let adults live their own lives as they themselves thought best, without interference even from parents, was followed faithfully by Shari mama and by my father who, albeit reluctantly, agreed with the principle.

(By the way, from now on I will refer to my father as Dadi; this name originated with Tommy whose first word was 'Dadi', spoken as he pointed at his Grandpa. From then on all of us, including Shari mama, called him this.)

The storm breaks out

April 1944 brought a tragic turn to the fate of Hungarian Jewry. The country was now occupied by Germany and the government taken over. The very first thing they introduced was the yellow star, which had to be worn by all Jews, irrespective of their religion – a Jew being defined as anyone with more than one grandparent of Jewish origin. A curfew for the Jews was also announced. Even with the yellow star we were only allowed in the street for a limited number of hours each day; anyone found outside after curfew was arrested and never seen again. The Jewish population of Budapest was forced to concentrate in houses marked by the yellow Star of David, if necessary moving from their homes to do so. Neither my parents' house nor ours had been marked in this way and therefore we had to move out and leave a good deal of our furniture and other belongings behind.

There was one incident I will never forget. I was helping to pack at my parents' place when the family from the floor below came up and asked us to let them look around. 'It will be very convenient for my son's family to move into,' the lady said, 'and I want to see how their furniture would fit in.' It was said matter-of-factly, without a trace of compassion or emotion; she saw nothing odd in the fact that a neighbour of six years' standing should be made to leave home; the only thing that interested her was the advantage to her own family. (Eventually, however, it was not her son who went to live there: when my parents moved out another couple, made homeless by bombing, was installed.)

Our little flat was also left behind and we all crowded in with Edith whose apartment was in a house marked with a star. It was a squeeze but at least we were all from the same family, without outsiders. My Uncle Pali and his family also moved to the same house with some other friends of ours. Altogether there were fifteen adults, one baby and Tommy, who was eighteen months old. Except for the mothers of the small children, we all had some job allocated to us, to be done during the time we were permitted to spend outside the house.

One day Shari mama, Uncle Pali and Aunt Manci were

summoned to the Gestapo headquarters. We were very frightened, of course, but it turned out that they were wanted for a special task – that of looking after the crowded houses in the ghetto area. This was a small area where *all* the houses were marked by the yellow star and because it was very overcrowded there was great chaos; the sanitation had become inadequate and the Germans were afraid that an epidemic might break out and spread from there to other places. Hence they had summoned a few people who they knew had done voluntary social work in slum conditions and commissioned them to care for cleanliness and order in the ghetto. Extra time was required to carry out this duty and they therefore received a pass allowing them an extension to the curfew.

It was a beautiful summer. Little Tommy, pixie-like with his suntan and curly golden hair, ran naked around the garden soaking up the maximum of the city's sunshine. A neighbour, whom we knew to be a regular churchgoer, complained and threatened to denounce the house for allowing such indecent exposure of a little boy. This sort of insult, from a so-called Christian, came like a cold shower to George and me. We cared less about atrocities from Nazi sources than about this. How could we uphold the validity of Christianity if its adherents behave in such a way?

The news from the provinces was becoming more and more alarming. Edith's parents were put in a train with many others – destination unknown – and so were all Jews, gradually, apart from those in Budapest who were apparently being left until last, the final chapter in the liquidation of the Jews. We knew that enclosed trains were rolling through minor railway stations and from the locked goods carriages came cries for help that could be heard in nearby houses. Where, we wondered, were those thousands taken? Old, young, children and even babies! For what purpose? Was that 'Auschwitz' that we had heard about the terminal for all of them? And when would our turn come?

We had to live with this permanent grief for our loved

ones and with the death sentence looming over our own heads. The repeated air raids we hardly cared about. Indeed, one felt safer during air attacks when everybody had to sit in the cellars of houses or in air raid shelters. During the bombing spells there was no extra molestation for Jews and we all thought that dying quickly during an air raid would not be the worst of fates.

In those days it was the daily visit of Dr Groh, a professor in medicine, that gave us the greatest comfort. He lived in a nearby street with his wife and six children and neither he nor any of his family had previously been a personal friend of ours. The only connection between us was that years ago he had bought the timber for his house from Dadi's timber yard.

When Dr Groh realized that one of the neighbouring streets contained a marked house he popped in to ask whether any of the Jews there needed medical attention. Then he discovered that he knew my father and from that day forward he never left for home from his job at the University without calling in to see that all was well with us. The Grohs were faithful catholics; in conversation he mentioned that the statue of Saint Margaret, erected in the front garden of a nearby catholic grammar school for girls, had been modelled after his eldest daughter. The statue was exquisitely beautiful and we imagined that his daughter must be an exceptionally charming girl. Dr Groh's faithful visits touched us all and it was a short time later that he and his family restored in us all our confidence in true Christians.

It was Tommy's second birthday, 15 October 1944. We awoke to a glorious morning, warm and bright. On the midday news there was a breath-taking announcement: the Regent, Miklos Horthy, had approached the Allied Powers asking for a separate peace treaty. Negotiations had already started and all laws restricting Jews were invalidated.

We could not believe our ears. I danced around with Tommy in my arms, singing, 'It is the nicest birthday present for you, little one, and for us all.' However, we did not yet dare to remove the yellow star from the house. It was Dr Groh, when he visited us soon after, who jubilantly removed the star and declared: 'My dear friends, you are free.'

Only a couple of hours later, however, came another announcement: the Regent had been made to abdicate because he had 'betrayed' the Axis powers to whom Hungary belonged. The Hungarian Nazi Party had taken over and its notorious leader was now in full command. All Jewish restrictions were fully valid, until further notice.

This tragic turn of events after such a joyful day devastated us all. We thought that events leading towards the complete extermination of us all would now move even more quickly. Apparently Dr Groh was of the same mind. Later that night he came again: 'My friends, the war cannot last too long now but the days to come will be very crucial. Under no circumstances can you stay in this house any longer. Later tonight all of you, all fifteen plus the two little ones, will come over to our house. We will hide you there,' he said reassuringly.

'But Doctor, you expose yourself and your family to immense danger if this is found out,' said Dadi, 'we cannot take that responsibility. And besides, to feed fifteen mouths in the present food shortage! No, we cannot accept your offer.'

'Now, this is my concern and not yours. I know what I am doing. Think of the young people and of the children, you must try to save them,' the Doctor said firmly. With tears in our eyes we finally agreed. Around midnight, when all the roads were completely deserted and there was no light from any source because of the feared air raids, all fifteen of us with the children (who had each been given a sleeping pill beforehand to keep them silent) tiptoed to the next street where a side door was left open for us. When we were all in and the door had closed behind us the light went on and there stood the sweetest apparition: Mrs Groh, a plumpish grey-haired lady, with laughing brown eyes, looking like an angel. She opened her arms and kissed us one by one, saying: 'Be welcome, my dear ones, the Lord has brought you here.'

At this moment, so moving, I suddenly remembered the night of our engagement. Then, my father had acted correctly yet cautiously; until he had made certain of his and his family's safety, he had not allowed the couple who had turned up into his house. But in the present situation the Grohs were risking all, their lives and their children's lives, and were proving that they 'loved their neighbours as themselves'.

One very big room was prepared for all of us, with mattresses on the floor; the shutters were closed, of course, and we were instructed not to open them, even in the daytime. However, we could use all the other rooms when there were no strangers in the house. Should the bell indicate the arrival of a visitor we must immediately retire into our own room and not leave it until we were given the signal to do so. Of course, we gladly agreed to these precautions.

Next day we were given breakfast and all the following meals – and so it went on for eight days. It was quite fun sometimes, hiding whilst friends of the Grohs, one or two of them of high priestly rank, visited the family and we held our breath in our own room. Sometimes not only our breath but other things too! A potty was provided for Tommy but all the others had to wait, often for a couple of hours, before being able to use the toilet.

Dr Groh became more and more downhearted. The expected change for the better did not come. On the contrary, notices were posted requiring that all Jewish men and women under the age of fifty should report on a given day to a certain racecourse from where they would be taken to various destinations. Furthermore, the scattered houses marked by the Star of David could no longer remain Jewish: all Jews had to move to the ghetto area. This seemed an impossibility as the ghetto was overcrowded already, yet this was the command.

Dr Groh did not wish to let us go but we all decided that we could not continue to place his family at risk. The following night, therefore, at midnight, we crept as before into the street to return to our own house and prepare for our destiny: my parents to go somewhere with Edith and Tommy and we, the young ones, to be taken who knew where. Our moving this time was easy; no furniture vans, no suitcases, just a rucksack with the minimum amount of clothing. In mine I carried a bulky edition of the Bible I did not want to part with, which I had received from Edith. Only a few weeks before she had presented me with this precious Bible. She had recently seemed less opposed to our faith and had been very impressed by the loving and selfless conduct of the Groh family.

The idea of death was close to us all. I hurriedly wrote a letter which I left with a Gentile neighbour, asking her to hand it to George should he survive the holocaust and not I.

Lives terminated – lives preserved

The morning came and George was the first to leave for the racecourse. We all hoped that his condition as war disabled would help him but this time it did not work. His steel corset did not move any hearts. Along with the other young men he was commanded to go on foot to the Austrian border.

I was luckier. Because I was a seamstress I was allocated to a group of Jewish women working in a synagogue building. Sewing machines had been installed and our job was to mend torn uniforms. We were kept there day and night, fed as little as possible, and had to sleep on the floor.

In those critical days Raoul Wallenberg, a diplomat attached to the Swedish embassy in Budapest, initiated a scheme to save as many Jewish lives as possible. The Swedish embassy started to issue protective passports in the hope that those in possession of such papers, issued by a neutral country, would escape the general fate and the passport would be respected according to international law. This practice was soon followed by the embassy of another neutral country, Switzerland. Protective signs were also issued by the Swedish and Swiss Red Cross organizations and placed on some of the houses previously marked by the Jewish Star outside the ghetto area hoping that those living there would escape the pogroms that seemed to be becoming inevitable.

The house where my Aunt Manci and Uncle Feri were living became one of those protected by the Swedish Red Cross. It was in Pest, on the other side of the Danube, and my parents and Edith moved in there. There was a faint hope that the inhabitants of those houses would be spared.

There were masses of people queuing up for the individual protective passports and it seemed impossible to obtain one quickly enough to save George from the fate of many young men who were now being murdered everywhere in droves, in those last days before the inevitable collapse of the German army. No more trains to Auschwitz: the machine guns made a quicker job.

Shari mama was the one who, with her permit to stay out of the house longer, undertook to queue up until she obtained the protective passport for George. But once it was in her hands how could she send it to him? She had a daring idea. Removing her yellow star, she went straight to George's office and asked for his director.

'What do you want to see him about?' she was asked.

'It's private,' she said boldly.

'Your name?'

'Tell him I am George's mother-in-law.' She was hoping the director would understand which George she meant. He did, and after receiving Shari mama very cordially, offered his help. He had a friend in the police who would be able to leave with the document immediately. He would travel the main road in his police car and call out George's name each time he came across a group of forced labour campers. The chances of finding George were slim but he would try.

By some miracle George and the police officer met and the passport was handed over. With this in his pocket George took a chance on escaping during the night. Crawling first amongst huge cabbages he managed to reach a minor road where he hitched a lift to Budapest – after, of course, removing the star from his coat.

After some trouble he found out where my parents were living and rang their doorbell. Shari mama answered and asked what he wanted without recognizing him. However, after a bath and a meal he was more himself again. But what was he to do next? Passport or no, a young man was not safe anywhere, especially not after escaping from the German command.

At this crucial moment Mary rang and asked if there was anything she could do for them. For the time being she and Emil had a free movement permit, which had been obtained for them by the Calvinist Church to enable them to work among Hebrew Christians. When she heard of George's plight she immediately offered to have us both in their home for a while.

Imagine my surprise when I chanced to look up from my sewing in the synagogue hall and saw Shari mama signalling to me from the door. I went to greet her and she whispered: 'George is back and safe at Mary's place. Try to sneak out at lunchtime through the back door. Take off your star, don't look frightened, just walk out naturally, take a tram and go to Mary's place yourself.'

To meet George again at Mary's place was like a wonderful dream. Was it possible that henceforth we might be able to face the future together?

Mary and Emil's flat looked like a refugee camp. We were not the only ones taking refuge there while looking for a longer-term solution. Every night we were joined by more of Mary's 'strays'. She disguised herself as a red-cross sister, wearing a big white head-dress and, with the help of a friendly ambulance driver, managed to transport people or bring them from Jewish houses on a stretcher, to be hidden in her own home. If they had been found out it would certainly have cost them their lives.

The number of Jewish Christians needing help was growing daily. The church, therefore, commissioned Mary and Emil and a few prominent Hebrew Christians to find premises and organize homes especially for the care of children separated from their parents or for mothers and babies. Several big houses stood empty, their occupants abroad, and a few were reopened for this purpose after receiving the protective shield from the Swedish Red Cross.

We spent about a week in Mary and Emil's flat and when they moved into one of these houses; we went with them to help run the place. A few other adult workers were also installed and soon the children and mothers started to pour in. Before we knew it the villa we occupied was accommodating 150 souls. It was the home of a titled family who had left behind some valuable antique pieces of furniture which, together with the Venetian chandeliers and silk wall coverings, spoke of a long-gone luxury. The big reception rooms were now used as dormitories.

George and I and another couple on the staff shared a little room, a former boudoir, with cherry coloured silk wall coverings. There was nothing else in the room but a mattress for each couple to sleep on. Laughingly we put down our rucksacks, with the remainder of our belongings, finding the situation quite paradoxical.

George looked after the administration of the place and registered the newcomers while I played with the children to keep them occupied during the day. I wore a white head-dress like a nurse, with a red cross, to look really professional. Two ladies worked in the kitchen and Mary and Emil liaised between the Red Cross, the church and the home. Nobody else was supposed to leave the place at all, in order to avoid drawing the neighbourhood's attention to the fact that a crowd of Jews was finding refuge there. Later on, after the siege of Budapest had begun, Mary alone ventured out daily in her uniform, a rucksack on her back, collecting food wherever she could find anything edible and available and then carrying it home for the other 150 of us.

It was also the responsibility of Emil and Mary to provide us with our spiritual food which was more necessary than even natural food. Each morning and evening we read the Bible together and many of the young mothers and the older children came to the Lord in those days. Amongst them was Edith, who had temporarily moved in with Tommy, and we thus came even closer together now that we could share a common faith.

A Hebrew Christian brother repeatedly visited us in the home. Imre was a man in his fifties, and he came to preach to us from quite a distance regardless of the dangerous situation on the roads. Brave like Mary and Emil, he not only ventured the journey himself but brought along his charming sixteen year old daughter, Anna. Sometimes I saw them through the window as they calmly approached the house, from time to time finding refuge in a doorway while shots whistled over their heads. They seemed unruffled. Imre had been a well known theatre director, a journalist and the author of a few books and had led a very worldly life before he and his wife Rozal, and his two children Janos and Anna, were converted. Since then he had devoted his life to studying the Scriptures and had been used lately for teaching and preaching, for both of which he had a great gift.

Telephone calls still came and went between members of our family until Christmas. Christmas Eve was the last night we spent upstairs in the house and we celebrated it as best we could in the circumstances.

Next morning, looking out from the window, I noticed that Hungarian Nazi troops had surrounded the building opposite which we knew to be a Jewish orphanage. All the children and their tutors were dragged out and led away. Horrified, I wondered where they could have been taken now that the Russian army stood at the gates of Budapest and all transportation from the capital had ceased to exist.

We soon got the answer. This was Christmas Day 1944. Shari mama phoned: 'My dear,' she said, 'I have very sad news for you and you must be brave and strong to comfort others and not break down yourself.' And this was what she told me: 'Last night the Hungarian Nazis behaved as if all the devils in hell were let loose. They surrounded several protected houses, ignored the Swedish or Swiss protective signs and dragged people out, then drove them to the banks of the Danube, shot them dead and threw the bodies into the partly frozen river. Some of the women they thought too weak to swim were thrown alive into the icy water presuming they would freeze to death anyway.'

Dreadful . . . terrible . . . I did not know what to say and suddenly it dawned on me where the little boys from the house opposite had been taken.

'I haven't finished yet,' said Shari mama in an unusually hoarse voice, and slowly she listed those of the victims who were our dear ones: 'Auntie Erzsi, Uncle Arthur, their son Gyuri, Nushi's father-in-law, an uncle and aunt of George (the parents of the two cousins we had in the home with us), George's grandmother and his mother.' I stood speechless, unable to grasp its full horror.

'But there is one miracle I have left until last to give some comfort to you both,' Shari mama continued. 'Ilonka mama was one of the women they threw into the Danube alive. What happened then she herself cannot recollect but she started to swim and managed to reach the steps leading from the Houses of Parliament down to the river, perhaps half a mile downstream. She staggered out from among the iceblocks and hid under the dark arcades above the steps. There she was found by a police patrolman who felt compassion toward the shivering elderly woman and escorted her, wrapped in his cloak, to the Swiss embassy, where she was given clothing and hot drinks and asked whom they should contact on her behalf.'

'She gave our address and fell into a half-conscious state of exhaustion. I went to collect her and she was soon recovered enough to be taken to our place. Luckily we are not too far from the embassy.' At this point the telephone line went dead before I could ask any questions; it was too much to take in anyway. I had to break the tragic news to George and to the two boys.

The younger one was eleven and his brother thirteen – how would they take it? Would they ever recover from this dreadful shock? When I finally managed to tell them the news we all felt so numb that it was some time before we could even cry. But, perhaps because the threat of death was always with us we were able to accept it with resignation and face the tragedies of our nearest and dearest. We were not alone, we shared the common fate of all other Jews in Europe.

The next night, after Christmas Day, the artillery bombardment became so heavy that we felt we would have to move the whole household into the cellars. Although these were quite roomy, previously used for wine and coal, 150 people were packed like sardines in a box and most slept with their head on the nearest available shoulder. I did not fancy such conditions and we carried on sleeping as before, on our mattress in the boudoir. Then one evening George insisted on our moving down ourselves. He said, 'Look, it is written that one should not tempt God. We cannot expect him to give us extra protection just because we don't fancy going down into the cellar with everyone else.' I was reluctant; I hated the filth and the smell down there, yet somehow did not dare to oppose him.

Next morning I went upstairs to wash some underwear and to take a change of clothes from my rucksack which I had left on the mattress. I found it riddled through and through with dozens of bullet holes.

The same day a friend came to take Edith and Tommy to a hiding place that seemed safer and though it was hard to part we were relieved to know they were in a better place.

The six weeks that followed Christmas were a nightmare. There was no more food in the house and no civilians were permitted in the streets at all. One day two nazis arrived and said that somebody had informed them of Jews hidden in the house; they would now report it, return with more soldiers and take us all away. When they left our cellar we heard a big explosion and later, when we peeped out, we saw their torn bodies in the front garden. This time we had escaped, but for how long? We knew who had given us away. A young Hungarian nazi living next door had continually blackmailed us with various threats. He knew the truth but wanted us to buy his silence. Until Christmas we gave him food, coal all that we had. Now that our stock was finished he had no more reason to keep silent.

Gradually we could hear the Russian guns getting closer and closer and German and Russian soldiers were fighting hand-to-hand in the streets. The nazis had to save their own skins now and thus the threat to us personally, as Jews, was reduced but we still did not know exactly what was happening outside our cellar. We knew that the house had been hit several times from the earpiercing explosions and the shaking of the building.

Inside the cellar a routine had been worked out. In the morning, after prayers, everybody received their daily portion of 'food', consisting of a handful of roasted barley. Some snow was collected from the backyard and, when melted, given out as drink. (Pipes and drainage systems were all burst and broken.) How the mothers who nursed their babies managed to give them any milk at all was another miracle. However, so far everybody was surviving.

We had a lady doctor on the staff who specialized in lung diseases. She gave a little medical help when necessary. Our main concern, however, was for a young pregnant woman whose baby was due any day. The doctor said that she was not willing to act as midwife in the present disastrous circumstances, without facilities and in front of 150 onlookers. Still, we were shut in and God alone could help in such a situation. Every time we had our morning or evening prayers we included a supplication on the pregnant woman's behalf that the Lord might keep her womb closed.

There were endless hours when we just sat in the cellar with nothing to do. We still had a few candles and I was able to read the Bible, or read it to others to find and give comfort. At many places, in my very bulky Hungarian Bible, the drops of wax still mark the chapters most often read.

Then one day a German soldier knocked on our door. We saw immediately that he posed us no threat. The man was totally exhausted. He fell down and asked for water. We gave him a little melted snow. He drank and went on his way with fear and sorrow in his eyes. We knew then that the end of the siege was in sight. This was my last glimpse of the feared Germans.

'Liberated' and counting the cost

Next day our cellar door was opened. There, framed by the winter sunshine with the glittering snow in the background, stood a Russian soldier. We were 'liberated' – our ordeal was over! Or at least so we thought. There was jubilation, shouts of joy and in the midst of the chaos of merry voices our pregnant lady cried out with her first labour pains. But this no longer posed a problem. Mary took her to the nearest hospital, only a few hundred yards from the home. Though the streets were littered with bodies of soldiers and horses no more fighting took place, at least not in our vicinity.

We all went upstairs but were appalled at what we found. There were big gaps in the walls, all the windows were broken; the house looked like old ruins. It was the coldest part of the winter, minus 25° by day and even colder by night. We could not possibly stay upstairs until some repairs had been made so back we went into the stinking but at least warmer cellar. Evening came and with it a new horror.

The same young Nazi who had blackmailed us for weeks now entered the cellar; instead of his earlier armband with the swastika he now had one that was plain red, and behind him came two Russian soldiers. The young man pointed to the women and all three giggled. The Russians wanted women and the young fellow wanted to do them a favour so he had brought them to a place where there were quite a few women together, unprotected. He hoped in this way to curry favour with the Russians in case someone betrayed his previous Nazi activities.

The Russian soldiers had big torches in their hands and went round the cellar looking into all our faces, picking out some of the women they fancied and making them stand to one side. They said something in Russian amongst themselves, then pointed to Emil, George and the two other men, indicating that they should follow them into the yard.

I noticed that Emil was very pale and gave Mary a kiss as if to say goodbye. We knew Emil understood Russian, having been in a Russian prison camp for some years during and after the first world war. What on earth was going to happen?

At this moment our cellar door opened again. This time a high-ranking Russian officer appeared, looking much more civilized, and spoke to us in perfect French: 'Ladies and Gentlemen, I am the commander of this area and my headquarters are next door. If you have any problems, just call on me.' It sounded like a message from heaven. The privates who had wanted to take our men and some of the women sneaked out, crawling on their tummies like serpents, making their escape as quickly and quietly as possible.

We learned the full truth later. Emil said that the soldiers had wanted to shoot our men in the yard and then come back to have fun with the girls. Another miraculous intervention had saved us at the last moment. However, as a precaution against similar incidents being repeated we women disguised ourselves to look as old and as ugly as possible, not too difficult when we were near skeletons anyway.

A couple of days later the cellar door was opened yet again and there stood Dadi, looking old and unshaven, with Shari mama in tears. When they realized that we were alive the relief brought more and more tears from all of us. 'This is the second time we have come,' Dadi said. 'Yesterday we made the long walk from our place, picking our way slowly amongst the debris, but at the end of your road, when we caught sight of the house, we had not the heart to come further. We thought nobody could be alive under this ruin of a building.'

'I just couldn't face any more,' Shari mama added, 'but today we made the attempt again and here – I made you a few little cookies from the last handful of flour we had in the house.' When we had calmed down, and gulped the first food we had had for weeks, we told one another all that had happened. Thank God, Edith and Tommy had been well looked after in their last hiding place and Ilonka mama had recovered and was well, staying with my parents.

'And what happened to Nushi and Laci (her husband), and Marika (Nushi's younger sister),' I asked, 'you did not mention them in your last phone call; did they escape?' This was another fantastic story which we were now told in detail. They had all been staying in the house from which the other inhabitants, including Aunt Erzsi, Uncle Arthur, their son Gyuri and Laci's father had been taken away and killed. It so happened that Nushi and Laci went upstairs from the shelter for some nappies for their baby, leaving it for a few minutes – they thought – in young Marika's arms. While they were up in the flat everyone in the cellar was commanded to come out and made to march towards the river. Nushi and Laci saw this from the window and jumped out into the backyard. They thus escaped and also saved Marika's life for a young nazi, seeing such a young girl (she was only sixteen) with a baby, took pity on her and secretly signed to her to step out of the line. From the whole house, she and the baby (and Nushi and Laci) were the only survivors. However, it was days before Nushi and Marika managed to find one another by sending messages here, there and everywhere. By then the baby was very ill, not having been nursed as before and,' Shari mama added, 'she is still in a critical condition.' Uncle Henrik, Aunt Lica's husband, had been shot dead as he fell over when driven from another house. This was the toll so far – of the ones they knew about.

In the face of all these tragedies we were amazed and grateful to have found one another alive. 'But what next?' was the question. 'Where shall we live until the Buda district is also liberated and we can claim our homes back?'

Shari mama said 'Ilonka mama has invited us all to their house to live in her own apartment. This flat, together with that of her mother's (George's grandmother) and the one where her brother and family (that of the two boys) had lived before are now also vacant and in those three flats there will be room for everybody, the whole family, at least temporarily.'

'Well, we can't join you yet,' George said, 'we must stay here, repair the house and wait for the husbands of the young mothers to return and fetch them, and the parents to collect the children in our charge. Then, when the home is empty, we will move out too.'

'But, of course, we'll come and visit you as often as possible,' I added. And so we parted again.

The main problem now involved feeding 150 people. I noticed women going to the frozen bodies of horses and carving meat from them – so, I thought, why not do the same? I took a long sharp knife and a big bowl and embarked on my very first attempt at butchering. It went quite well and I returned to the home with a huge amount of meat, out of which we made a large pot of soup: 'The most delicious soup and meat we have ever had,' said the children.

I repeated this exercise every day; the freezing temperature was an extra boon since it kept the horsemeat fresh under its cover of snow. But as many households were living this way the source of this 'delicacy' was soon exhausted.

George and Emil then went together to the countryside to hunt for food. Back they came two days later, rolling a barrel in front of them. It was a barrel of sauerkraut, raw and cold, yet it kept us going for some days. Gradually, in exchange for engagement rings and watches, one could obtain flour and potatoes from the peasants who brought their produce to the city to sell. This was how I lost my diamond ring.

'Never mind,' said Shari mama when I told her, 'my engagement ring had exactly the same fate after the first world war; and in any case, what better use can be made of jewellery than to exchange it for food in a crisis?'

But let me return to the 150 left in the home, mainly children but adults too. It was a miracle indeed that none of them – none of us – had died during the siege either under the crumbling building or from exposure to cold, or simply from starvation. But after the 'liberation', one little girl was found dead by her mother one morning. The girl was a victim of leukaemia. We wanted to spare the mother as much as possible, and undertook the necessary steps on her behalf. 'Steps' in this case must be interpreted literally: individual bodies had to be taken to a big burnt-out department store which had been turned into a morgue. It fell to me to take the child's body in a borrowed pram to this place. It was about twenty minutes walk from the home – a sinister journey, offering another opportunity for meditation about life and death, yet I was totally unprepared for the sight that met my eyes at the store. Military and civilian lorries were arriving, one after the other, loaded with corpses, just thrown one on top of the other, arms and legs hanging out, distorted faces uncovered. Yet, when I overcame the initial shock, an extraordinary peace took its place. I realized that the bodies were nothing but empty vessels; the souls that had departed from them contained their personalities and they carried on existing in a world beyond our present perception. What was precious in each of those people – faith, hope and love – would never cease but live for ever. Somehow it was not the indescribable horror of the sight that stayed with me but the peace that God gave me in that tragic situation.

Next day another, less sinister, journey had to be undertaken from the children's home. This time George and I were pulling a little cart carrying as many children as the wheels would bear. We took them to the nearest delousing station to get rid of the lice in their hair and clothing. We trotted on to the primitive delousing institution; some little girls left their attractive hairstyles (and their hair) behind. Anyone seeing us leave with little boys and girls and returning with 'boys' only might have wondered where all the girls had gone! The trip was a great source of jokes and laughter; for us it was an hilarious experience: to trot next to one another, literally yoked together like a pair of horses!

Meanwhile the repairs to the home went on as best they could without materials or workmen. We stuck paper into the empty windowframes and cleaned up the toilets – a job that I undertook. It was quite a task as the toilets had been neglected and without water for weeks. Even so, I still remember the satisfaction I felt when they were sparkling white again! How right Shari mama had been when she had told me on many occasions that any job can give satisfaction if carried out well. Cleaning loos can also be a joy, I thought, as I added my own discovery to her lesson.

The relatives of the children – and of the mothers – now began to turn up. What scenes of joy we witnessed every day! Still, much anguish had to be shared with those for whom nobody came. 'Maybe tomorrow your daddy or mummy will come too,' we tried to comfort them, but hope faded for some as the weeks went by. Finally, however, we found homes for all the children. If the parents did not appear, relatives took care of them temporarily, until they could be transferred to a new home for Hebrew-Christian orphans which opened, with foreign aid, under the auspices of the Calvinist Church; Mary and Emil were its leaders.

As to our personal list of losses it was gradually completed from information coming from various sources. The list that I now reproduce includes the names of close family members only.

Close relatives lost

Name	*Note*	*Relationship*
Aunt Erzsi	shot into the Danube	my aunt, Shari mama's sister
Uncle Arthur	shot into the Danube	my uncle, Erzsi's husband
Gyuri	shot into the Danube	son of Aunt Erzsi and Uncle Arthur
Judith	starved in the ghetto	my cousin Nusi's baby daughter
Uncle Henrik	shot on the wayside	my uncle, Aunt Lica's husband
Zsuzsi	gassed in Auschwitz	my cousin, Aunt Lica's daughter
Erika	gassed in Auschwitz	Zsuzsi's daughter
Jeno	burnt alive in barracks	my cousin's husband, Aunt Lica's son-in-law
Imre	died in forced labour	my uncle, Lola's (Shari mama's sister) husband, Marci's father
Uncle Lakatos	gassed in Auschwitz	my sister-in-law Edith's father
Aunt Lakatos	gassed in Auschwitz	Edith's mother
Grandmother	shot into the Danube	George's grandmother
Bela	shot into the Danube	George's uncle, father of boys with us in the home
Teri	shot into the Danube	Bela's wife
Fate yet unknown in 1945		
Bandi		my brother

New life from the ruins

At last the day came when we were free to take up our rucksacks and move into Ilonka mama's house, where most of the rest of the family had already found temporary refuge. Nushi and Laci and Marika were also living in one of the apartments and when I met Nushi for the first time after her very heavy losses I could have wept to see her once mischievous face so lined with sorrow. 'And the little baby has died too,' she said, resignedly, without tears. I felt unable to say anything. I just embraced her. We were, however, amazed to see how Ilonka mama had regained her strength and energy. She was acting as mother to the two young cousins and this responsibility was keeping her going.

We found my parents rather oddly occupied in the yard and although we laughed we were rather proud of them. They were both working hard, standing face to face, holding the opposite ends of a saw in their hands and cutting wood. Half burnt doors and discarded broken furniture were the 'raw materials' they were using to obtain fuel for heating.

'Do you need such a huge amount?' we asked, puzzled by the large heap of wood already cut. 'Ah, but this is not only for us: we have started to sell some as well.' Thus, Dadi, who not so long ago had owned a prosperous business, acres of woods and machines, and who had employed workers and clerks, restarted his working life in these humble conditions with Shari mama, the ever faithful companion in all his enterprises, at his side.

The retiring German army, in order to slow down the Russian advance, had destroyed all the bridges across the Danube in their wake. They also went on defending the hilly parts of Buda for another few weeks, although their situation was by now hopeless. However, the day came when communications between Pest and Buda were restored by the erection of an improvised wooden bridge.

We went first to see our flat, or rather we went in search of it. In its place was a gaping hole. Nothing was left of it, it was a complete ruin. Our furniture, my trousseau, all our expensive sets of blankets and lingerie practically unpacked and unused by us had gone, and I didn't even care, so little did it seem to matter.

Edith's flat, which we had left with just our rucksacks, was still standing but completely empty. Edith's and Shari mama's household stuff, their dresses, everything, had been taken away. Some of the neighbours, thinking that we would never come back, had just helped themselves and we were told that most of the rest had been taken away by Hungarian nazis and the retiring Germans. However, a few pieces of furniture were returned to us when the more honest of our neighbours saw that we had survived after all.

My parents' flat was quite habitable and when they returned to it the couple who had occupied it could have been required by law to leave. All Jews had the right to reoccupy their original homes automatically, without having to put in a claim. My parents, however, did something which I consider unprecedented. Because the couple installed in their home had nowhere to go, they allowed them to stay and share their home with them. 'Well, my dear,' Shari mama said to me, 'it was only recently that we were ourselves homeless. One should not forget these experiences. It was terrible for us and it would be the same for these poor people.' So the five of them (including Dadi's sister Lica, by now a widow) started to live under the same roof, in a flat of no great proportions, sharing a kitchen and a bathroom – very trying circumstances as anyone who has ever attempted to live this way would agree. Yet, somehow, it worked out tolerably well. Later on, under the communist régime, many flats had parts forcibly allocated to strangers, often creating a hellish situation in which housewives nearly killed each other over cookers and bathtubs. But in my parents' house there was always peace and order although the man they shared with took to drinking and was sometimes very noisy. God had indeed given my parents an extra dose of grace and patience. For them this situation lasted for another eleven years, until 1956.

One of our most shattering experiences came when we visited the Groh family. The part of the big house where we had hidden, the actual corner, was a heap of rubble. Under it, still buried, was the body of Groh's beautiful daughter, Matild. A heavy bomb had hit the corner of the house and the stones had buried her. Her body had not yet been recovered. As we stood there, stunned and speechless, totally bewildered, Mrs Groh turned to us with a sorrowful yet sweet smile: 'The Lord gave her, the Lord took her away, blessed be the name of the Lord.' There was no bitterness. They never asked, 'Why did it happen to us who helped others in a manner not many dared to do, who have always been good churchgoers and lived an honourable life?'

Dadi provided all the materials needed for the restoration of their house; we felt that this was the least we could do after what they had done for us. Yet they never took even this small favour for granted.

Later on, after Dr Groh's death, Mrs Groh went to live with one of her daughters and whenever we met her she mentioned Dadi's good deed. The last time I saw her, while visiting Budapest in 1977, she was suffering badly from arthritis yet her bright dark eyes still shone with the light of those who have joy and peace in the Lord. She was happy to hear that all our children had become believers but seemed especially delighted when I spoke of the conversion of Shari mama. 'You see, my dear, I have prayed for your precious parents every day. I knew God would reward them for all the goodness in their hearts.' My words of gratitude to her, so much more deserved, she just brushed aside, 'It was my neighbourly duty, my dear, not worth mentioning.'

Those of our family who had survived went to work as

soon as possible. Those who had had a job 'before' carried on with it; others started afresh. We all hoped that our country had finally taken the road to freedom and democracy.

George returned to his previous job where he was given a splendid welcome, for he had always been popular there. Dadi found his timberyard deserted, all the stock burnt and the office building ruined. However, the site was still his so he began work again, albeit on a very small scale. I went back to work as a seamstress in the workshop of a wholesaler of ready-made dresses, both George and I hoping that we could now think about starting a family. Edith found herself a job too, so Shari mama devoted her full time and attention to Tommy. Even many years later, when he was at school, Tommy went to Shari mama every weekday, had a meal and did his homework until Edith returned from her office.

Some social and political issues

In the autumn of 1945 George's firm – a big company operating coalmines, cement factories, power stations and so on – decided that its head office employees ought to be more in touch with the workers in order to improve industrial relations. In the past there had been little link between them. The administrators in Budapest hardly ever went to the mines or the factories and the workers had never seen the office at headquarters. (Even on the spot, where the mines were, there was small contact between the workers and the white collar employees, the distinction between them being quite sharp.) In the new post-war world, Hungary was more socially aware than ever before (with the exception of the few months of communist régime in 1919) and it seemed vital to break the class barriers.

A two-day excursion was organized from Budapest for the central staff to visit the coalminers; they would spend the day sightseeing and the night in one of the miners' houses, with the miner's family.

This was a tremendous experience that has had considerable impact on our thinking ever since. For a part of one day, and for one night, we had direct insight into the life of workers under an extreme capitalist system, a system which still reflected the prewar situation since changes were only just beginning and the old ways were still in existence.

The local offices were neat and clean. In contrast, the facilities enjoyed by the workers were neglected. Even though the company was making considerable profit not much was spent on welfare. There were many examples of discrimination, of the inferior treatment of the workforce compared with that of the white collar employees. However, the real shock came when we were eventually taken to our hosts for the night. We had been allocated to a miner who lived in a small house, in a row of similar houses, which had neither sanitation nor any other comfort. The street was a mere muddy road with ditches at either side which had to be stepped over in order to approach the house. Mud and sewage mingled together into a sticky substance in the ditch where children were playing. Obviously those who were too lazy to go to the latrine behind the house had used the ditch instead.

Our host was a nice man. He described himself as a real socialist and said he had spent several years abroad with his family, as a miner in Belgium. 'You see,' he said, 'in the West they have unions who care for the workers' welfare. In this country so far there has been no organization to defend our rights. In Belgium we were given a three-bedroomed house with all the facilities and a social worker visited regularly to check on cleanliness and to make sure that each child had a separate bedroom. Now come inside and see this shambles'.

We entered the house and his wife, a kindly woman, met us and showed us around. The house, or rather hut, had one bedroom and a kitchen which was also used for eating in. That was all except for a latrine at the back. 'Two couples live here,' she said, 'we two, and my son and his wife.'

'But there is only one double bed in your bedroom,' I said in amazement. 'Where does the other couple sleep?'

'Oh, that's organized,' replied the miner's wife. 'The young couple work the nightshift and my husband the dayshift; when we get up they go to bed.'

We shared this well-used bed with the older couple for the night. The two men, the miner and George, slept on either side of the miner's wife and myself. The bedlinen was slightly dirty and smelly but I couldn't feel sorry for myself while others had permanently to live in such conditions.

'It won't be long before everything changes,' said the miner next morning at the breakfast table. 'You may be wondering why I came back from Belgium where we lived as princes compared to this. I felt I should not be selfish and turn my back on my fellow workers here. We came back to help build a just and socialist country where all have equal rights to live a normal life.'

It was one thing to hear from Shari mama of conditions in the slums and quite another to experience them ourselves, if only for one day and night. We developed a keener sense of social justice after this visit and realized the necessity of legal protection for those who are abused by others in authority over them. It was the first time we understood the role which unions could, if run properly, play in the defence of the labour force.

How could this situation be possible in a so-called Christian country like Hungary where, before the war, most people had attended church regularly? Had the industrialists, factory directors and landowners never heard the commandment to love your neighbour? Or was it that they did not consider the underprivileged to be their neighbours and therefore took no responsibility for them? A change was obviously inevitable and, indeed, necessary. But would it come slowly and democratically or would it involve another drastic upheaval in which the innocent would surely suffer along with the guilty?

We wanted to turn our backs on the past and concentrate on the present and the future. Our aim was to rebuild a normal existence with normal incomes. None of us could predict that the present democratic political situation would be only temporary, merely a time of transition. We knew nothing of the background forces already preparing for a totalitarian takeover with the aid of Soviet Russia. The contents of the Yalta agreement, made between Stalin, Roosevelt and Churchill with the intent of influencing the political and economic development of the countries they had occupied during the war, were not made public. Thus, for three years, we lived in ignorance, under the mistaken belief that Hungary was building up a western-type democratic system. Only gradually did it dawn on us that this was not happening.

Even during those 'democratic' years life was not altogether easy. There was galloping inflation, which rose at an unprecedented rate. Everyone was paid weekly and on pay day one had to buy all the non-perishable goods for the week ahead since only one day later the money would not have sufficed. Anything left over had to be invested at once in pieces of gold because by the next day, or even by the same evening, the money would have lost half its value. All the street corners had stalls where gold was available. Small pieces were preferable, perhaps just a few grammes clipped off a chain or a necklace, as these were easier to exchange as the daily food supply needed to be replenished. This situation was a feature of the first seven months of 1946, although inflation had begun immediately after 'liberation', stabilizing only after the introduction of the forint in August of that year.

Joy and Sorrow

Mary Hajos and I became pregnant at the same time. This was a most odd situation since I was twenty-two and she was forty-two. Their joy was just as great as ours but to them it was a tremendous surprise, for they had been married for a long time without children. The regular Bible studies had now begun again in their home as before and the number of people finding God through their ministry was running into hundreds. We sometimes wondered, in fact, how Mary would be able to carry on with her work when her child was born. However, Mary's life seemed ordained to be spent in the service of God alone; her baby was born prematurely and died within three days. Although it naturally caused Mary and Emil great sorrow, we knew that their ministry would benefit by their experience. Why then did God give them this baby in the first place? This question had many of us puzzled but Mary herself supplied the answer. Perhaps the experience of pregnancy was necessary to complete her personality so that she would understand other women in the same situation. 'And when we arrive in heaven our little girl will welcome us there and we will rejoice together,' she said, closing the subject for ever, peacefully and even gratefully.

While I was pregnant we were offered a flat in the block where George's office was located. It was a good and comfortable home and we moved in, leaving one room unfurnished for the use of our baby. Shari mama came with me to the hospital when my labour started and stayed with me in my private room all night and the next day, until late that night when my first son Jani (John) was born. I stayed in the hospital for two weeks, receiving masses of flowers and visitors and being spoilt by everyone. This continued for six weeks at home with Shari mama and Ilonka mama coming on alternate days to relieve me of all housework so that I could have a happy, restful time with the baby.

We invited Mary and Emil to be Jani's godparents and

with their acceptance we became even closer. Jani certainly could not have had more faithful godparents and they followed all the details of our lives with the greatest interest, not confining themselves merely to Jani's spiritual welfare. This interest continues even now since Mary is still one of our best friends.

When Jani was only five months old I became pregnant again, this time unplanned. When summer of 1947 arrived Jani was just about starting to walk, although he was still faster on his knees. He was quite a handful, moving swiftly from room to room, first hiding under the piano then creeping to yet another hiding place, but he was very sweet indeed.

At about this time the first prisoners of war returned from the Russian camps and we were in daily expectation of seeing Bandi again. One day I went to see Edith and found her sobbing on her bed, Shari mama sitting with her arm around her, also in tears. I knew before they told me. The news had come through a friend of Bandi who had been with him in the Russian prison camp when he died of complete exhaustion following lack of food and weeks of exposure to freezing weather. Once again I was struck dumb, unable to find words of comfort.

At this point Dadi arrived, having been notified by telephone at his office and asked to come to Edith straight away. When he heard the news he fell on his face, flat on the floor, sobbing and shouting, 'No sons, none, Bandi is also gone.' Shari mama tried to comfort him, asking him to consider Edith's feelings and to compose himself for my sake in case the upset brought on a premature birth. As always, Shari mama overcame her own heartbreak, her consideration for others being stronger than her own grief.

We had to accept this tragic loss and to add one more name to our list of losses, this time of our nearest and dearest.

Our grief was beyond description and, of course, the hardest hit was Edith. She carried on bravely, living and working for Tommy's sake, feeling that the sole remaining aim of her life was to bring up her child in the best possible way. Her standards were very high and she was very ambitious for her son to become outstanding in all respects. Sometimes she was perhaps stricter than other mothers because she was trying to be both mother and father to Tommy. My parents were a great support to her and Tommy provided a source of joy in the midst of sorrow.

I admired Shari mama's self-discipline, yet some symptoms betrayed her inner sorrow. She no longer held herself erect and the asymmetry of her back became more and more obvious. Her fingers were gradually deformed by arthritis and she suffered from angina. This often caused pain and pressure on her heart which she tried to hide, taking her little white tablets in secret.

Just before the birth of my second child, Edith's brother, Bundy, arrived on a visit from England. It was a great comfort to Edith to have at least one of her immediate family left. Bundy told us fantastic stories about his war years. He had been at Dunkirk and it was from him that we first heard details of that historic event. From all his accounts we were most impressed by the incredible care taken in the British army over every individual soldier which contrasted so strongly with our own war experience. Britain seemed like heaven to us, a place where the rights of the individual had more respect than in many continental countries.

Bundy tried to persuade us all, especially Edith, to come and live in England. With our grief so fresh in our minds, however, none of us had the heart to make such plans. When he returned to England though, he made us promise to think about his invitation and to seriously consider emigration. 'I am not yet rich enough to buy the island, the one I promised you before I left Hungary for good,' he said jokingly, 'but I earn enough to be able to look after you all for a while until you can make your own way.' None of us dreamed then that we would ever take up his offer.

Our second son was born in August 1947 and we named him Andrew after Bandi, my brother – Andi for short. Imre and his wife Rozal were his godparents. We had a very close relationship with them, just as we did with Emil and Mary and we enjoyed so much the company of these two older couples. Their wisdom and experience seemed inexhaustible and even today, decades later, we find ourselves quoting their views on the bringing up of children or any other matter.

1948-1956
Snippets of private lives and political events

In the summer of 1948 there was a general election. None of the individual political parties obtained a majority but the hastily arranged coalition of the social-democratic and communist parties managed to do so and formed a government. Very soon after this a purge was started in the social-democratic party with all moderate elements either dismissed or arrested. Any remaining left-wingers joined the communists so that there was eventually only one party in power. This was led by Matyas Rakosi, the notoriously doctrinaire Stalinist, who became prime minister and head of the party.

The new order now began to infiltrate all aspects of our life. We were continually under observation, our movements registered and our telephones bugged and every word spoken in public reported. This situation, of course, required a large amount of controlling and a secret police was established. In the work place also 'reliable' party members were recruited to 'report' to the party secretary in whose office files were kept on each employee. This file contained information of all kinds, including one's origin (worker, peasant, middle class or upper class), political views, religious attitudes and so on. We lived in a goldfish bowl, continually aware that all we did or said, or even believed, was known and could be used against us at any time, whenever it pleased the party officials to arrest us as dangerous persons. We had now become suspect as 'bourgeois' elements, no longer for being Jewish, and again had to endure persecution.

One day an official delegation visited Dadi's office. They came to tell him that his firm had been nationalized. They then asked for all his keys, including that of his office safe, and commanded that he leave the premises for good. This was the end of his career as a businessman, and also of his business, for ever. There was, of course, no compensation, unlike the Western practice where owners of nationalized firms are at least given some payment for their property. Nor was he employed by the newly created firm but expected to look after himself. He was remembered only at the end of the next financial year when he was given a tax demand on what he had earned prior to nationalization. No one cared that he had no means of paying this tax except by selling his personal belongings.

Financial loss left my parents amazingly indifferent. 'Once a son is gone, someone you have brought up and loved only to be taken from you, what do material goods matter?' Shari mama used to say.

My father was not a man to be overcome by circumstance, however. He found himself a job in a construction firm and from this humble beginning soon began to make a name for himself. Before long he was reported in the newspapers for his innovative ideas which had saved considerable sums of money in the building and construction industries. (I still have cuttings with photographs showing him alongside the scaffolding of his own ingenious design.) Reluctantly, his bosses did acknowledge his worth and even endowed him with honours, awarded to him by the very system that had previously made him a pauper! He was by this time already in his sixties, when people usually retire, but there were still new phases of his working life ahead of him.

Shari mama also began to branch out on new activities.

She offered her services for Jewish welfare work on a voluntary basis, visiting people and reporting on their circumstances in order to obtain financial or other help for the needy.

One of her most remarkable cases involved an old gentleman called Mr Majorosi, an orthodox Jew. Shari mama, to her amazement, had found a most peculiar situation. When she called the old man was in bed, unshaven, with his little skullcap on his head and with him in the apartment were his wife and her two children. The lady looked much younger and her features were definitely non-Jewish. 'Let me present you to my wife, Countess X, and her children from her first marriage,' he said. 'She was widowed after the war and married me. I was able to look after the family quite well until recently, but now that private trade has ceased my livelihood has also come to an end. Believe me, Madam, I can do business with anything – if I am allowed!'

'But you seem to be bedridden,' said Shari mama, 'what is the matter with you?'

'Well, I have to confess to you, dear lady, that I am not ill. I had to pawn my suit when my money ran out and now I have to stay in bed until we can afford to reclaim it.'

That problem was easily remedied, my mother giving him the 'quick aid' she often paid out in similar circumstances, and she asked him to call and see her the following day.

Shari mama told me the full story the next day. Mr M appeared, freshly shaven, smartly dressed, full of new energy and reassured her that she had given him new life from a growing depression. A small but regular amount of help was then secured for the old man but he soon found a way to buy and sell goods privately again. Many of our belongings were sold through old Uncle M, as we called him, as the need arose to supplement our meagre income.

Uncle M grew very fond of us and said that he prayed for us every day, forgiving even the 'tragic' fact that George and I had left behind the religion of our ancestors: 'To people who have such a mother even this sin is forgiven,' he used to tell me.

Like all others, George's company had been nationalized in 1948 and he had been transferred to the Ministry of Building to deal with factories producing bricks. At first he was not too unhappy but later on life became more and more difficult. He was made responsible for too much that was outside his power to control and when things went wrong his boss threatened him with various unpleasant prospects including the secret police. George lost pounds and pounds of weight under the strain but this was not the only difficulty. At the close of office hours the staff were supposed to stay on for various activities arranged by the party for everyone, party members or no. There were meetings of all kinds including brainwashing lectures and social activities, all aimed at curtailing private life.

In 1949 I became pregnant again. Jani was at this time still sitting on a seat fitted to Andi's pram and we began to wonder how we would cope with a third baby in our fourth floor flat with its dangerous small balcony. I had been taking the boys daily to a nearby park but was not sure I could do this with three little ones. One day we received a notification from the office which already occupied two floors of our block. They now required the entire building and all tenants were to leave within one month. They did, however, pledge themselves to cover the cost of removals and also to provide the 'key money' we would require to obtain another flat. Despite the financial help it proved to be very difficult to find a new flat. There was a severe shortage of accommodation in the capital because of a large movement from the country to the city and new houses had not been built in sufficient number to provide for the influx. One month was very short notice and we knew that only a miracle could help.

After three weeks of unsuccessful flat-hunting we were, indeed, given a miracle! We heard of a family house, once belonging to a rich dentist and now converted into two flats. The ground floor apartment with its back garden was about to become vacant. It was a lovely flat, almost too beautiful, with huge rooms, a porcelain fireplace, wood-panelled ceilings, huge sliding glass doors dividing the rooms and a little fountain on a wide terrace from which stone steps led down to the secluded garden. To move into such an elegant place seemed to us to be provoking fate and at first we refused it. 'If the party ever sent anyone to visit us they would assume that we were and still are very rich, otherwise we could not possibly afford such a home. This flat is not for us,' said George. However, the month neared its end and no other flat was available so we had no choice and we moved in.

When our friends came to see us we apologized for our embarrassingly posh home. We disguised the fountain by planting geraniums in it but that was about all we could do to reduce the overpowering effect! But God knew why he had presented us with this spacious home. Very soon it began to fill up as new laws forced more and more people into less and less space. The first to come were Ilonka mama and George's orphan younger cousin, who she was now looking after. (Miki's older brother had emigrated to Israel.) The next to come was Marci, my cousin, who had married and needed accommodation. One of our rooms was quite self-contained, with a little kitchen, and the young couple moved in there. The flat was still roomy and comfortable enough for all of us to live there.

Soon after we moved in Julie was born. We were delighted since we had hoped for a girl this time, after the two boys. Her christening was held in the big lounge of our new home and a minister friend came to conduct it, in the presence of family and friends.

Our new home provided a graceful background to this unique occasion. But what a trick fate was playing on us, we thought! Just as wealth, and even the impression of wealth, was held to be a disgrace, here were we landed with the sort of accommodation most suited to grand social events. We didn't want it nor were we able to afford it! George's income was barely enough to cover the cost of our food. Although he wrote some textbooks and some magazine articles to supplement his salary, we had regularly to sell bits of our remaining valuables to make ends meet.

As the children grew and started to attend kindergarten I began to think about working again. George suggested that I should learn something interesting in order to have a more satisfactory occupation than sewing. I trained for a few months, therefore, in architectural drawing and afterwards got a job in a big planning office, where I worked on the design of industrial buildings. From then on our financial situation eased somewhat. Ilonka mama was able to relieve me of most of my housework and she also took the children to the kindergarten every morning and picked them up every afternoon at four o'clock. When I returned from my office I was free to play with them, give them their tea and their bath, and put them to bed.

During these years we went on Sunday mornings to one of the churches nearby or to one whose preacher we wanted to hear. There was no membership system and the congregation hardly knew one another. The children came with us and sat through the service since there was no Sunday school. We tried to explain the sermon to them afterwards and they took it in quite remarkably well. This and my regular little Bible studies were their only spiritual food. We ourselves learnt most from the midweek Bible studies held at Mary and Emil's house and at the meetings of a group of younger couples who met at Imre and Rozal's on Saturday nights. There we found true fellowship combined with friendship and excellent teaching since both Emil and Imre were outstanding biblical scholars.

This period, after we had recovered from the war and after the children had passed their most demanding phase, gave us the first opportunity in our own lives to really think about ourselves and our spiritual needs. Up to then, as 'innocent victims' of the nazis our recognition of Christ had focused on him as the Redeemer, who had to die to save the wicked, the warmongers, those who were just indifferent, and so on. The world would become a better place if only *they* would accept and apply Jesus' teachings. Gradually, however, in the light of what we were now reading and hearing and because we could now observe the lives of our maturer friends, we were starting to see ourselves in a new way. We now aimed at a much higher standard of conduct than before but, to our alarm, realized that we could not achieve it. Our moral upbringing could not provide a strong enough foundation for such aims, nor could it help us to fix our sights on what Christ had proclaimed as righteous living. The higher were our requirements, the more we failed them. Humbly, then, we recognized that we also needed forgiveness. This is how we began to know Jesus as our personal saviour and were comforted by the promise of the forgiving love of the heavenly Father.

In 1951, at the height of the Stalinist era, the Hungarian government decided to purge the capital of all 'enemies of the socialist system', in other words, all previously well-to-do and influential people. Industrialists, businessmen, politicians, intellectuals, aristocrats, were all put on a blacklist and received orders by special messenger to vacate their homes within forty-eight hours. They were allocated rooms in villages, sharing the homes of peasant families. Neither those who had to move out nor those who had to take them in were consulted about these arrangements. Orders were simply given out and the police made sure they were obeyed without opposition. Once again there was daily agony: would Shari mama and Dadi be on the list and, if so, when would their marching orders come?

One morning, they came. With resignation Shari mama began to pack their belongings. We were in despair since news of those already 'in exile' was alarming. Some were living in a room with just a dirt floor and without any means of heating. The peasant families understandably hated those who had been forced upon them. To put under the same roof such totally different lifestyles, cultural backgrounds, levels of intelligence and standards of cleanliness was totally absurd and could not possibly work.

Would my parents once again be evicted from the home that they had so willingly shared with the couple installed in it by the nazis? This seemed a grave injustice to me, something that, from God's point of view, made no moral sense at all. No it can't happen, God will surely intervene! Whilst we were praying, Dadi informed his office that he would have to leave Budapest in two days' time and so would have to resign from his job.

The remaining hours passed quickly and suitcases were filled with the minimum amount of clothing, kitchenware and bed linen. All was now ready for the lorry that would pick them up the next day. We were very upset but Shari mama tried to comfort us. 'As others have survived this ordeal so will we; God has helped us in worse situations and will do so again.'

Late that night, just before going to bed in their home for what they thought was the last time, and when I myself was near despair, the doorbell rang. In the doorway stood the union secretary from Dadi's company. 'Comrade Leimdorfer (everyone was called a 'comrade' in those days), here is an official withdrawal of the order you received yesterday. You are permitted to stay here and we hope you will continue in your job with the same courage and inventiveness you have shown so far. And now have a peaceful night, your worries are over.' With that he shook Dadi's hand and went.

Our gratitude to God for his intervention through those who appreciated Dadi's work, produced an odd mixture of emotions. We hugged and kissed, laughing and crying at the same time. We wanted to help them unpack but Shari mama sent us home. 'Go and calm down and have a good night's sleep yourselves. I will do the unpacking tomorrow and I assure you it will be the most enjoyable work I have ever undertaken. So please leave this pleasure to me.'

1953 brought change and an easing in the political situation. Stalin died early that year and after his death things became more moderate. It was a relief to be free of some of the past threats and to hope that conditions might improve day by day. In 1954, our dear Ilonka mama died very suddenly from a stroke that proved fatal within minutes. This shock and sorrow drew our attention away from the political scene for a while. There were, however, a few political ups and downs in the years between 1953 and 1956. In the summer of 1956 Dadi received yet another prize for his latest innovations. This was a holiday, to be taken with Shari mama, in one of the big hotels run by the unions. It was a great honour and they looked forward to it very much. It was fixed for 15 October. The resort was in a hill forest area and therefore promised to be very beautiful with the trees resplendent in their autumn colours. As for Shari mama, two weeks with no cooking and no other household or family duties, offered a fantastic prospect. They left on schedule.

Second act: last scene

On 23 October 1956 the revolution broke out.

I do not want to go into great detail since the world knows how the desire for freedom suddenly broke bounds and became an irresistible force. Enthusiastic young men, students and children were joined by the rest of the population and even by the army itself. In those few days of hope and euphoria people suddenly became sacrificial and super-honest. Money was collected for various altruistic purposes in open bags in the streets, left uncovered and unguarded overnight only to be filled up even more the next day. Strangers smiled at one another and there were no grumbles in the food queues. Our country was to become a free democracy, so we hoped, after decades of totalitarian oppression of one sort or another.

However, after the first few days we began to hear alarming news. Some people had taken justice into their own hands; some secret policemen were hanged in front of their homes.

Various parties, some from the extreme right, were rapidly organizing themselves and were hoping to get a substantial number of votes in case of a free general election. Landowners from the earlier régime announced openly on the radio that they expected to have their lands returned to them, land that had been distributed amongst the peasantry after the war. The former rich were in grcat haste to grab back what had been theirs before.

Despite this, we hoped that common sense would prevail and that Western statesmen might help us to work out a balanced and free democratic system. We listened again regularly to the BBC, hoping for some encouragement, advice or directive. Alas, there was no such thing. It was then that we were made aware, by the Western broadcasting services, of the treaty of Yalta, when Roosevelt, Churchill and Stalin had decided the fate of Europe between them. Hungary, together with the other countries of what has come to be called Eastern Europe, had been allocated to the Russians. They were our overlords; we were in the Soviet orbit. The Western powers promised to help with food parcels or clothing but in no other way. It was clear that our struggle for freedom was doomed from the start; yet we hoped for a miracle. Maybe the Soviet government, headed now by Khruschev would grant our country a new beginning seeing that it was the wish of the majority.

When Shari mama and Dadi finally managed to get home from their holiday, they told us some revealing stories of what was going on there. 'The first few days, before the revolution, I was shown a cold shoulder by many of the other holidaymakers who were mostly party members. I even overheard them calling me a bourgeois and they pulled faces behind my back, asking each other how on earth had I got to this place, since it was meant for 'real' workers. But the day after 23 October some of these party members suddenly became great patriots, sounding off with right-wing slogans and calling me a 'dirty Jew'. I had thought I would never hear this again but there it was, the old dormant anti-semitism revived at the very first opportunity. This country has not changed and we will never be accepted as one of them, whatever the régime,' Dadi commented sadly.

Five o'clock in the morning on 4 November the well-known sound of heavy artillery fire woke us up. We put on the wireless. Imre Nagy, the prime minister of those few 'free' days, was speaking. He left us in no doubt about what was happening. His tragic voice informed us that the Russian army was advancing towards the capital and he repeated his SOS cry to the West.

The children were wide awake and very frightened; we dressed them quickly and went down to the cellar for protection against the barrage that sounded as if it was on our doorstep. For a few days we spent most of our time sitting on top of the heap of coal stored for the central heating, listening to the BBC to find out what was happening. (We had no faith in the communist propaganda from our own local station.)

There was no doubt – it was all over. The cause of the revolution was lost. On the Hungarian radio the people's uprising was already being referred to as the 'counter-revolution' initiated by 'reactionary' elements and instigated by the Western 'imperialistic and capitalist' powers. It was the old story repeated again. How long could we stand it? After the few days of hope it seemed especially tragic and unbearable to return to where we had started in 1949.

After a few days in the cellar we heard the gunfire die down. We ventured up to find all the windowpanes broken but otherwise no damage to our home. However, Shari mama and Dadi's place was uninhabitable and so they moved in with us temporarily, until it could eventually be rebuilt.

'If only we could escape from this country,' sighed George. And soon we heard that many had had the same idea and taken flight over the Austrian border, where the Hungarian army was turning a blind eye to this extraordinary phenomenon. Many thousands crossed the frontier that way with only a bundle in their hands or a rucksack on their back.

One day Bundy, Edith's brother, phoned from London. His message was brief. British visas were ready for the whole family. If we could manage to get to Vienna, he would take care of the rest. Edith and Tommy did not hesitate for long. They went off, together with a friend of the family, Gyuri Schustek and his two children. He was a widower and was in love with Edith who was hesitating over accepting his marriage proposal. In this crucial situation, however, it helped to make the dangerous journey together. Their party had to sneak over the Austrian border overnight, in snowy and icy conditions.

We, on the other hand, did not dare to embark on such a journey with our much smaller three children, who might not be able to walk for miles. 'If God wants us to go,' I said, 'he will perform another miracle as he has so many times before and he can take us over the border on eagle's wings or by normal train, possibly even in a sleeping car, in comfort and without any risk or danger.' I also felt that I could in no circumstances leave my aged parents behind. When Bundy phoned again to reassure us that Edith and her party had arrived safely in London and urged us to come I told him that this seemed most unlikely, because of my parents. 'But my dear,' he shouted into the phone, 'I told you the visas were ready for all of you, including them; I knew you would never wish to leave them so I requested visas for them too.' We were deeply moved by this generosity and so one of the obstacles had been removed. I wondered how God would respond to the other, absurd challenge of mine.

We applied for an emigration passport. Humanly speaking there was no hope that we would be granted one. Old and retired people obtained emigration documents in exceptional cases but there was no precedent at all for young families being permitted to leave the country. George stated that he was war disabled, whereupon the authorities answered that they would consider our application. At least they did not refuse it outright.

One day Imre and Rozal came to see us. Imre asked how matters were going in connection with our planned emigration. 'Wc haven't heard any further word at all about it,' George said.

'Well, if you still want to go, maybe somebody we know can help you obtain your documents.' Imre then told us about one of his friends, a very influential man, who had to move into the capital from a provincial town and needed a bigger flat for his family, one where he could receive officials. It has to be a 'representative' home. Ours might be just right. He would mention it to him and see his reaction.

Within days all was arranged. So then we understood the full significance of God's providence in letting us have such a beautiful home seven years ago. Our passports were granted and we started to prepare for this major step – maybe the biggest in our lives – of leaving the country. The children were very excited; for them it was a great adventure. They assured us that they wanted to go, despite the difficulties we warned them about. But underneath the excitement we were, of course, very sad to leave everybody and everything behind.

Luckily, there was little time left for thinking. We planned that my parents (who obtained their passports relatively easily, as old people) should follow a few weeks later, giving us time to settle in a bit. Good old Uncle Majorosi undertook the sale of our furniture and carpets. It was quite an emotional strain to see our beloved items disappear one by one. They went for a pittance but we needed the money to buy proper outfits for us all so that at least in the first few years we would not have to spend on these things in the new country.

A man from the National Museum came to inspect our silverware, pictures and china and gave us permission to take them with us since they were not 'national treasures'! Also, we were summoned to sign documents renouncing our rights to any property or estates that might be in our name.

The days were filled by these and similar events. They ran by swiftly – but not the nights. Sometimes I woke up as if from a nightmare. Did we really have to go? I thought I would never bear the parting – it is very hard to cut oneself off from friends, relations, a beautiful city where one has been brought up. But then I considered the courage of my parents and felt ashamed of my weakness. For them, it was much harder, for they were leaving sisters and brother behind. Though still active and agile, Dadi was past seventy. Would he be able to work in order not to become a burden on anyone? – that was their main concern. For people of their age to move just from one house to another is an upheaval but my parents were willing to move to another country, to an unknown destiny, into another world with another language that Shari mama spoke a little and Dadi even less. But they never complained, never showed anxiety, instead gave us support and advice in all our doings.

'Wherever you live will have to become our home too; we know that you would never leave us behind and we do not want to become a factor hindering your decision. The rest is in God's hands.' This is what they told us and never wavered in their determination.

Our departure grew nearer. We planned first to go to Vienna where we wanted to visit friends. From there we would go to Switzerland where Mary and Emil were staying. Emil was convalescing there after a major infection that had proved obstinate to treatment. More thorough examinations revealed that he had a type of leukaemia which was, humanly speaking, fatal. However, he had improved slightly and it was hoped that a longer stay in that healthy climate might arrest his illness. He was perfectly at peace and accepted whatever the Lord had planned for him, either the termination of his life or, by miraculous healing the restoration of his health.

After a few days of rest in their blessed company we were to carry on with our journey to England. On Emil's recommendation we received a very cordial invitation from the Hebrew-Christian Alliance of Great Britain to stay in their guest house in Kent until we found accommodation and employment.

All seemed taken care of and well thought out but during our last few days in Budapest news came from Edith that she was unwell; there was something wrong with her chest and she had been taken to hospital. This was worrying news yet we hoped that her condition was not serious. Edith was married by now to Gyuri Schustek and surely he would take good care of her, whilst the three children, Tommy and Gyuri's two, Ferko and Marika, were being looked after by Bundy and his wife. All must be under control we hoped.

The farewells were heartbreaking. Eventually the day came when we shut the door of our home behind us for the last time. We had asked that no one should come and see us off at the railway station because a tearful departure would have been more than I could have endured. It was evening when we boarded our sleeping carriage about which I had told endless stories to the children beforehand so that they now climbed into their berths with enthusiasm, clutching dolls and teddies. Slowly, the train was set in motion, speeding us into a new and unknown phase of our life.

We did not go to bed before we reached the frontier as we had been warned that we had to undergo a very thorough examination. So it was. We had to leave the train, and were shown into a small station where I was undressed by a woman border guard (and George by a man). After this we were allowed to dress again and rejoin the children who had been left to sleep as a very great favour by the militia. Minutes later there was another leavetaking, this time from the country where we had been born and brought up, where much joy and much sorrow had marked our years.

The axe has done its job severing our roots. Yet, it did not cut us off from past memories – these we took along with us as lifelong companions.

Once on Austrian soil we went to have a brief rest ourselves. When he kissed me goodnight George said: 'On eagle's wings or in a sleeping car; that is what you said, isn't it?' And we knew for sure that we were in our Lord's gracious hands for the unknown future.

PART III

TRANSPLANTED

Landed

The crossing was calm. When the white cliffs of Dover came in sight we stood on the windswept deck, in the bitter cold, gazing at our new homeland. What sort of life awaited us? How would we cope with the language? My own lessons with Mary had given me only a basic knowledge of English. George, however, had won a national competition at eighteen, so at least we felt we would be safe with him.

At Dover the porter said something to us and then rushed off with our luggage. 'What did he say?' I asked George.

'I haven't a clue,' came the reply.

'But surely you must understand, you learned English for many years.'

'But this porter spoke a different English, totally foreign to me,' said George in despair. However, eventually we found our porter on shore. We managed to leave our luggage at the station and went to have lunch.

In the little restaurant we were faced with another problem: ordering lunch. There was a handwritten menu and the names of the dishes were new to us. Eventually we discovered 'fish and chips' (well-known to us from our textbooks) and decided to try it after our soup. With a sigh of relief yet another hurdle was crossed. Then Julie asked me which was the soup spoon. We looked with amazement at the spoons in front of us that had shapes different to what we were used to. I tried to guess but I must have been wrong! The waitress giggled as we started to eat our soup with the pudding spoon.

'Apple pie with custard?' asked the girl when we had finished the fish.

'Custard? What is this?' I asked George.

'Some sort of vanilla sauce, I believe,' he said. 'The English put it on every pudding. Let's try it.' All tasted very good and life began to seem a bit more promising, despite the bill, which we found enormous. At any rate we had celebrated our arrival by eating the English way!

Soon we were bound, by train, for Ramsgate where we were expected at the guesthouse of the H.C.A. It was run by a couple of refugees from Germany so at least we were able to communicate in German, to our great relief. Once installed in our rooms, we went to have our first wash in England – in an icy bathroom.

'It's not usual to heat bathrooms here,' Mrs Anker informed us. 'You'll soon get used to it and it'll toughen up the children.'

So, gradually, we got used to the unheated bathrooms, to the lounge where the open fire warmed our fronts but left our backs shivering, and to all the unknown dishes. We went for a walk each day despite the east winds that nearly blew us off the clifftops. On these walks, the first daffodils, crocuses and wallflowers gave us courage: it was a display of nature's survival in this rough climate.

First impressions of Britain

Apart from feeling cold all the time, we were immensely impressed by the Britain of 1957. We were struck by the calm, the discipline, the courtesy in shops and the patience when queuing. Both adults and children were good-mannered, respected older people and were willing to assist one another in all situations of need. There was orderliness and stability. Very soon we had the most favourable encounter of all: education.

On our second day in Ramsgate we went to see the headmaster of a school. He was most encouraging. It was not all smooth going, however. The first day our children came home all worked up. 'We will never wear these clothes again, everybody laughed. They danced around us and looked at us as if we were monkeys in a zoo,' they shouted.

'Why, what do English children wear?' I asked.

'Short pants and not these ugly long trousers; and the girls have short skirts and socks. And they have lace-up shoes. Nobody wears booties as we do.'

And here we were with lovely, newly bought clothes and shoes, which had to be sent back to Hungary for other children. We had to buy everything from scratch. That was a blow to our very meagre finances but we felt we had to do it. It was hard enough for the children to go to a school where they were unable to follow the language – at least we could spare them ridicule on account of their clothes.

Every afternoon we studied with them, trying to teach them the language. It seemed to us hopeless: they would never be able to participate in their classwork. However, just as the headmaster had predicted, within six weeks they understood their lessons. So much was going on in those first few weeks that our attention was taken away from the children's progress and it was a real surprise when we discovered that they had overtaken us and were starting to correct our mistakes!

'. . . Thy rod and thy staff, they comfort me'

After a few days in Ramsgate we went up to London where Edith's brother Bundy met us at Victoria Station. The chaos of London seemed to us unbearable but luckily we were taken straight away by car to Bundy's house to meet his wife, Lilian, Edith's husband, Gyuri, Tommy, and his recently acquired stepbrother and stepsister.

'How is Edith?' was our first question.

'We hope she will be better soon but come and visit her with us this afternoon. She's eager to see you.'

We found her beautiful as always, but very weak. We chatted about everything and she asked me whether her children could join us at Ramsgate for the Easter holidays. We thought this was a good idea, the six children would have a lovely time together and she could rest a little longer in the hospital to get better. She turned her face towards the window as if she had tears in her eyes.

'It is so good to have you here,' she whispered. Then she quickly pulled out a little note from under her pillow and slipped it into my hand. 'Here, hide it and read it when you are alone,' she whispered.

We returned to Ramsgate the same day and Tommy, Ferko and Marika joined us two days later in expectation of much fun and games with us.

When I opened Edith's note I was stunned. She had written that despite hopes of improvement it was possible that she might be very ill: the doctors had told her that she would be operated on soon in order to find out what was really wrong. She wrote that if she did not survive the operation it was her definite wish and will that we should take Tommy into our care. She also hoped that we might be able to look after her husband's two children, at least temporarily, until he overcame his grief and settled down somewhere to provide a normal home for them. 'My brother and husband will certainly cover all your expenses but I know these children need a motherly heart to comfort them and to replace me. Lilian is a nice lady and did all she could to launch us in this country but she cannot be expected to have the same understanding in dealing with Tommy as you who have known him since he was born.'

Reading her note, we thought she must have exaggerated her condition; surely there could be nothing fatally wrong with her. After all, she had left Hungary only four months before a fit and healthy young woman. No – it was not possible. Yet, the afternoon of the operation Bundy phoned, sobbing into the phone: 'She is cancerous all over. They say she has barely a few days to live.'

'How is Mummy?' asked Tommy eagerly when we had finished our brief conversation.

'Not too well,' I said, to prepare him gradually for the grave situation about which he had no suspicion at all. 'It's more serious than the doctors thought.' On one of the following days I travelled up to London alone, leaving the children in George's care. I found Edith in great pain and obviously without the will to live.

'Do you want Tommy to come and visit you?' I asked her.

'For God's sake, no! He should always remember me as I was before and it will be easier for me to depart not seeing him again.' She knew the end was near and did not mind. That was the last time I saw her.

Next day George travelled to London and spent hours at her bedside, taking turns with Gyuri and Bundy, until she died two days later. When they phoned that evening to say that she was expected to pass away soon, Tommy, Ferko and I didn't go to bed. We sat on the beds in my room, talked, prayed or kept silence and waited for the call. It came in the early morning. Edith as she herself said, 'walked over into the other world.' She went in peace, strong in the Lord whom she had found and loved in the last years of her life.

The children took the news silently. Then Tommy asked us to leave him alone in his room for a while. By noon he had still not appeared. I wondered what was happening, but did not want to disturb him. At lunchtime he reappeared, calm and composed. We were all amazed. It was only years later that he told me about those few hours of solitude. 'You know, when I was confirmed in Budapest just before we left, I understood what the minister told us but only with my mind. But during those painful hours I experienced God's loving presence with me. It was absolutely real and he comforted me as only a father could.'

Indeed, only someone whom God comforts could have overcome such a blow in the way that Tommy did. Here he was, not quite fifteen, never having known his father and now losing his mother at this very sensitive age, in a new country and a new school where the language was alien to him, with no friends and no roots. Yet, at the end of his first school year in Britain he was first in all subjects in the A stream of a grammar school. Ferko, one year Tommy's senior, finished with the same outstanding result. We still have the local paper that reported the 'miraculous' results of the two Hungarian boys, 'miraculous' even to a reporter who was unaware of their tragic background. Yet with the help of the Lord it had all become possible.

My parents were absolutely heartbroken when we telephoned the news of Edith's death. Yet, it did not alter – indeed it strengthened – their decision to come and join us as soon as possible. Tommy was more like a son to them than a grandson and they, like us, felt that their place was near him. They therefore speeded up their preparations for the journey.

As Edith had wished, all three children – Tommy, Ferko and Marika – were to come under our care, with financial contributions from Bundy and Gyuri who, soon after the funeral, left this country and settled down in Austria. He was so grieved that it seemed more appropriate that his children should stay with us. So we started our new life with six children.

New job – new home – the house fills up

The number one task for George was to find a job. The second was to settle into a home where all ten of us (my parents, the six children and ourselves) might somehow start to shape our existence together. Both needs were very urgent. There was not much time left for grieving or for pondering the meaning behind recent experiences.

George wrote more than a hundred letters of application to various companies. He received kind and polite answers but they were all refusals. At one point it seemed impossible to obtain any job corresponding to his qualifications and ability. Finally, through the recommendation of a friend, a very junior and temporary job was offered to him in an economic research institute, something usually filled by a university student as a holiday job. It was offered to George because the Institute wanted to help a refugee at the time. A move to London now became even more urgent. We were encouraged by the Hebrew-Christian Alliance to buy a house and they themselves offered to arrange a mortgage for us. Bundy and Lilian did some househunting and, after a short while, phoned to say that they had found a place which they thought very suitable. When we saw the house we agreed with Bundy and Lilian that it seemed suitable and soon the deal was made. Only much later did we appreciate how perfectly suitable this choice had been. The position, the district, the schools, the local parks, the good transport facilties, all the things we were unable to evaluate for ourselves as foreigners in London, turned out to be just right for us.

We were given a date in May 1957 when we could move in. A couple of weeks before moving day my parents arrived in England and we went to Dover to meet them. There was sadness and joy, hugs and kisses, and much talking to catch up on the news we hadn't been able to communicate by letter or telephone. The train journey to London seemed to be over in no time at all. Bundy was faithfully waiting for us at Victoria Station with his car and he took us to some rented accommodation where my parents were to live until the completion of our house purchase. Dadi looked through the car window, bewildered. The traffic, the similarity of the streets as we crossed district after district, made him more and more uneasy. After Bundy had deposited us at their hired flat he burst helplessly into tears, 'Shari, I believe we have made a terrible mistake. We will never be able to find our way in this chaos of a town; we will not be able to leave our home and consequently not be able to find work. To be a burden to our children, this will be our fate.'

We comforted him and reassured him that we had felt exactly the same during our first days in London. We told him how we had gradually managed to find our way about and how we had got used to many aspects of this new country that had initially appeared so strange. As for a job, Bundy promised to employ Dadi in his factory to work in the packaging department, which might not be too strenuous for him.

'And I will look around to see whether there is a market for plastic flowers,' Shari mama said, matter-of-factly.

'What are you talking about?' we asked, never quite prepared for the surprises which Shari mama frequently presented us with. She explained that her cousin in Paris dealing in plastic flowers was willing to give her the agency for England. So in the hope of good prospects for both of them, we left to return to Ramsgate for another couple of weeks.

Within days their letters were assuring us that they were both getting around very well with the help of maps. Dadi had started his job and Shari mama had begun investigating possibilities for her little business and, on the whole, they had started to feel quite at home in London. Amazed by their letters, George said to me, 'I bet they will show us around in London by the time we move there!'

Finally the day of completion arrived. When our little van stopped at our vacant house, the neighbours, who discreetly observed our movements from behind their net curtains, were very puzzled indeed. First a few suitcases were unloaded, then some chests and then nothing. No beds, no furniture – nothing! Only people. We came first with our three children, then my parents arrived, then three more schoolchildren. 'Heavens, ten of them in that house! And where from? And how will they live without any furniture?' The neighbours later on confessed their surprise and we laughed about it together with them. That peaceful suburban street had not known anything like it.

The previous owners had left behind, for a token sum, a very old and worn-out three-piece suite and a dining table and chairs and so we were able to start our life in the house with somewhere to sit, eat and sleep. When I discovered that they had also left a bulb hanging in each room I felt truly grateful – we would have light on our first night! The beds were bought new, the first items we invested in, and they were delivered the same evening, as agreed.

When we sat around the table that first night, all ten of us, we said our prayers before the meal in tears. 'For what we have already received – and are going to receive – may the Lord make us truly thankful – his name be praised. Amen.'

Settling in

We settled into the house and bought good but second-hand furniture remarkably quickly. Using the money Bundy had lent us, we very soon found exactly what we wanted and the house looked homely after only a few weeks. Looking around our cosy sitting room, the old suite embellished with flowery loose covers and fresh curtains at the windows, we remembered the blessing of Uncle Majorosi. The last time he had come to us in Budapest, into the bare and empty flat that had once been a nice home, he asked permission to pray for us. I will never forget his shining face while he laid his hands on my head. The old Jew who revered his Lord reminded me of the Old Testament patriachs. He was obviously inspired when he uttered the words, 'God will bless you abundantly in the country where you are going; he will provide for you a comfortable place to live, a home as lovely as the one you are leaving behind . . ' Yes, the blessing had proved to be prophetic: it had become a reality. Our settling down was a smoother and easier task than we had ever anticipated when we first contemplated the drastic decision to emigrate.

The first Sunday, George and I went with the six children to the church at the corner of our road. It was our intention to try a few churches before finally settled in one of them but we felt at home straightaway in this Congregational Church. That first Sunday, the very first hymn was well known to us from Hungary: 'Praise be to God the Almighty, the King of creation . . .' and we sang happily with the congregation. Also, the minister spoke a clear English which we could fully understand. After the service we went to the vestry, introduced ourselves and were given a very hearty welcome by the minister, Keith. He soon visited us and has become a faithful friend. He used to pop in occasionally to chat with my parents who were very impressed by his kindness and his honest concern for them although he knew they were Jewish and did not belong to his flock. Shari mama particularly valued this greatly and started to come along to church with us, albeit not regularly as she did not want this to become a divisive issue between her and Dadi.

Our two boys joined the cubs, Marika the guides and Julie the brownies. Thus, it was in this church that our new roots began to take hold.

When we started to live together the ages of those in the house covered a very wide range: Dadi seventy-four, Shari mama sixty-six, George forty-two, myself thirty-four, Ferko sixteen, Tommy fifteen, Marika twelve, John eleven, Andrew nine and a half, and Julie seven. For our three children it was a new experience suddenly to have another two brothers and one sister – something they had to adapt to. In the very first week there was an emotional upset, caused by some triviality, that brought on tears. 'Mami, you are unfair; in every single matter you take the side of the older children as if they were always right and never us!' But this was their first and last complaint of this kind. I explained my motives: that we need to give special love to those who are not fortunate enough to live with their own parents. Especially now, at the beginning of their stay with us, they must be treated with special tact and care. This was immediately understood and accepted, tears were wiped away and soon the new situation became a delight for our children.

As to the newcomers, Marika was the one who had a hard time getting used to Julie, several years her junior, with whom she shared a room. Julie, who enjoyed having a new older sister, followed her everywhere, bombarding her with questions, yet (as Julie now looks back to those first months) Marika showed great patience with her. The two big boys, Ferko and Tommy, had few problems. Both of them were very independent and reliable youngsters who lived a way of life different from the others. They kept to their room for hours, doing their schoolwork, or played tennis; also, from time to time they helped the younger ones with their homework. Neither in this initial period nor at any time later did we have any problem with these two; our relationship with them was more that of friends. We stood by them when they needed our support but in turn they gave us a good deal of help and understanding. The fact that Tommy was a serious believer also had a great effect on our children. He was respected by them as an older brother and his example was much more beneficial than anything we parents could have said on the subject.

The main – and also the most difficult – adjustment to make must have been that of my parents. Only now that we approach their age group and are grandparents ourselves can I fully appreciate their endurance. To live under the same roof with six noisy children and have only a small bedroom for privacy must have been a tremendous strain on them. However, my parents never showed any strain or impatience; they took part in our joys and in our worries and were united with us in most aspects of life, from the beginning. They were indeed outstanding and remarkable people.

Shari mama started the agency selling plastic flowers. This meant that initially a great collection of samples arrived by post from France. These she arranged in a bouquet and went around from store to store, showing her collection to the buyers, taking the orders and importing more flowers from France. In those days there were no plastic flowers on the market; it was a novelty and for a while she was the only one who sold them in Britain. Soon a corner of our morning room was curtained off. Shelves were fixed on the walls, and on these Shari mama stored her incoming stock. At night, after dinner, Shari mama and Dadi spent hours sorting out the orders, writing proper invoices, keeping accounts and so on. This was Dadi's 'second shift' after having spent a full working day in Bundy's factory.

They were the ones who usually got up first in the morning. Shari mama prepared breakfast for all of us and only then did she start her journey to town with the flowers. Soon she knew London better than any of us. As she trudged wearily home in the afternoon we often noticed how bent her little figure had become, yet instead of having a rest she would emerge from her bedroom with an apron on, asking what she could do to help in the kitchen with the preparation of the evening meal. Never did she complain or betray disappointment and only years later did she once admit to me that often, after having been rudely treated by some arrogant buyer, she had had a good cry on the way home. But by the time she arrived she had always collected herself and got rid of her 'self-pity', as she called it.

After a few months George presented the work he had been temporarily employed to do. It was so well received that he got a further contract on a more permanent basis with a great jump in his initially very low salary. The research work also became more and more challenging and satisfying in this new capacity. Through him the Lord provided for us really abundantly and we never ever knew a lack of anything we needed.

In the first months of our stay in Britain I too found a job, in an architect's office just a few blocks away from our house. Soon I learned the English measurements and scales that were so different from the continental ones I had known in Hungary. I worked there for a year but when

George's institute introduced a new quarterly publication and was looking for a draughtsman to prepare the charts and diagrams I applied and obtained the job. I could do the drawings at home which was a great advantage, in view of the demands of our very big household.

Thus a normal pattern of life unfolded as everybody in the house settled into jobs and schools. The weekday routine was enlivened by social activities: young and old brought in their friends and it was considered an exceptionally quiet weekend when there were only the ten of us around! On holidays, birthdays and anniversaries there were real celebrations in which all the generations happily took part together. And so the years flew by, practically unnoticed, with the usual events of all child-raising families. When I now pick out from the sea of memories episodes that were characteristic of those years, whether they were at the time funny, moving or annoying, they have all become sweetened by the beautifying distance of time.

Terrible/tolerable teens

4.15 pm: The table is set for the children's afternoon tea. I stand at my bedroom window waiting for Demetrius to turn in from the main road. Demetrius is the name of a small Morris, vintage 1930 or so, that Tommy bought with Bundy's financial contribution. Its roof open, bottlegreen arms waving in all directions, tassels from the girls' hats floating behind, it now zooms into our road and pulls up at the house. The children spill out from the car, into the hall where they dump their cases, to take their seats at the table where they munch their endless slices of bread, butter and jam and report, possibly all at once, on their respective days at school.

Then they disappear into their study-bedrooms (two to each) and immediately turn on the radio or the recordplayer. A cacophony of rock music blares out from three directions. 'Music is stimulating, it helps us to concentrate on our homework' is the slogan, so how can one object? The older generation resigns itself and hopes for a better future when the musical tastes of the children might perhaps mature.

7.15 pm, dinnertime: I ring the bell, doors open, the stairs creak under the thunder of rushing feet. This is the time when all the members of the household gather together. The meal lasts a long time as all kinds of matters are discussed, political, ethical and so on, but this is not the last forum for solving the world's various problems.

Final discussions start at about 10.30 at night, after the grown-ups' bedtime. Then, with cups of cocoa, the children gather again in the morning room. Now, without the annoying wisdom of the older generation, they can readily put forward their revolutionary new ideas.

'Mummy, do you really want to come in and meet our friends? Do you insist?'

Yes, I did insist on making my appearance at their party, so they accepted it with a deep sigh.

I knew that my awkward accent was a great source of embarrassment to my children as it betrayed at once to their friends that we were foreigners. To reduce their unease I jokingly rehearsed beforehand, appearing with a tray in my hand and saying, 'Hello everybody, do you want your hot dogs with mustard or horse-radish sauce?'

We made our children blush whenever we opened our mouths in their school, in shops and in all other public places. This was ludicrous and sad at the same time. One could not help wondering whether it was right to leave one's birthplace behind, mainly for the sake of the children, and then become an embarrassment to them because of our 'inferior status' as immigrants. This situation changed as the children matured, however, and it changed drastically.

'Mami, please cook something Hungarian when my friend comes tomorrow; she loves exciting food and her mother only cooks very plain English dishes.'

'It is so different in our house from any of my friends' homes; even down to the furniture arrangements or the carpets – ours is so individual and so much more interesting.'

'Don't be embarrassed to speak, Mami, everybody says your accent is charming.'

These were the kind of comments that were made by the time the children were fifteen and over.

Once they had reconciled themselves to their background and developed their own identities, all the strain that had caused awkward moments in the past disappeared.

Sometimes I lost heart but when I shared my depression with Shari mama she used to say, 'Chin up and carry on, my dear.' With her wise evaluation of the situations and her apt comments she was a real comfort to me. Her comfort never boosted my self-pity and sometimes worked like a good, sobering cold shower. No wonder our children held her in high esteem. Even in their turbulent years, in the midst of their rebellion against all adults, Shari mama enjoyed their respect.

John was an ardent woman-hater in his adolescent years. 'I will never spend my time with stupid girls and will never get married – that's for sure,' he burst out furiously after a confrontation with Julie. Then, with a pensive expression and the slightest hint of a smile he added: 'Unless I have the good luck to find a woman like Shari mama.' I could hardly believe my ears. That a frail old grandma should represent a teenage womanhater's ideal was better proof than any words of Shari mama's exceptional personality. At the first opportunity alone with her I repeated John's words. She laughed but was very touched too.

I was a very affectionate yet a strong-minded mother who demanded a lot from the children. I was critical, not encouraging enough, quick tempered and interfering. I see this clearly now but while the children were growing up I made many mistakes, partly through ignorance and partly through not being able to change.

George provided one balancing factor and Shari mama the other. George was a father figure of the kind that made it easy for the children later on, when it came to their personal encounters with God, to relate to the heavenly Father. He was the image of reliability, security and loving care, yet he never imposed his advice or his help and never attempted to 'invade' the children's private thoughts and feelings. He was satisfied with, and enjoyed, what the children shared with him spontaneously. He gave them love with liberty.

The feminine virtues were represented in the family by Shari mama: femininity in the best sense of gentleness combined with strength of character, a rare combination. This became our children's ideal of womanhood. To prove that such an ideal can become reality, we had Shari mama.

. . .Great things he has done

Ferko was the first to leave home. He went to live in digs when he started college, reading mathematics. Tommy stayed with us throughout his student years, when he read physics at University College, London, and even during his postgraduate year when he studied for his Diploma in Education. After Ferko, Marika left to be trained in catering and hotel management.

Then in 1962 the incredible happened: Dadi retired, at the age of seventy-nine. Shari mama's flower business also had to close down. Plastic flowers from Japan and other Far Eastern countries had flooded the market and the French imports could not compete with them. She could not have carried on, in any case, as her back had become more and more bent, her arthritis more acute and the little white tablets that she took for her heart condition disappeared even more frequently under her tongue. We felt that they needed a place of their own, not too far away and yet separate from us. How this could be solved we had no idea. But God's providential care showed itself again and the solution came at just the right moment.

After the war the West German authorities had promised to compensate 'victims of nazism' (not Jews alone) for the consequences of persecution: loss of life of parents or children, health damage, material loss and so on. Soon after our arrival in Britain, Dadi had put in two claims, one on his own and one on Tommy's behalf. That had been years before and we had given up hope that anything would ever materialize. Yet, it did. During Tommy's first university year the verdict came through. Tommy received a fairly large sum in compensation and in addition a monthly amount was granted to him until he finished his education. It came as a great surprise. For Tommy, the best way to invest the lump sum was to buy property. Thus, he bought a flat just round the corner from us and Shari mama and Dadi moved into it.

They enjoyed their little garden very much and Dadi worked hard to keep it tidy. But he carried on looking after our garden too, even after they moved away, walking over to our house every single day, partly to do some gardening but also for a good chat, sharing all our concerns including those of the children.

One of the most precious days in Dadi's and Shari mama's life was Tommy's graduation day in 1964. This occasion was of particular significance to my parents. They sat in the huge auditorium of the Albert Hall and listened to the endless list of graduates. Tommy was one of them. What a wonderful moment it was to hear his name mentioned, graduating in Physics with first class honours, to see him going forward to the stage and shaking hands with the Queen Mother. These moments, I am sure, compensated them for the many hardships and losses they had endured.

After the ceremony a small family party carried on the

celebrations. Tommy had recently got engaged and we had tea together with Valerie, his fiancée, and her parents, who had come up from Dorset for their daughter's graduation. Many photos were taken of the two of them in their gowns – both looking so smart and Valerie very charming. Then at tea we began to get acquainted with her parents. This was another milestone in our family history: the beginning of the 'nest building' of the third generation. It also had extra significance in that we would now become closely related to an English family and our new roots further embedded in this country.

The transplant seemed to be succeeding.

When we left Hungary nobody had thought that it would be possible in future for relatives and friends to obtain passports for travelling abroad. We had been prepared never to see them again. But as the system in Hungary took a milder turn a stream of visitors came to see both of us and, of course, London. After my parents' and then our generation, the younger ones soon started to flock to London, those who had still been children when we had left Hungary. They came mainly to learn English in the summer vacation and also to tour Britain. In the summer months our house began to take on the appearance of a, sometimes overbooked, guesthouse.

Apart from the burden of the quite considerable extra work, it was, of course, delightful to see old friends and have them in our house. My parents were particularly pleased to see their close relatives again and proudly showed them around their beloved London.

One of our most cherished visitors was Mary Hajos. After Emil's death she had left Hungary to start a most remarkable new phase of her life. She had settled in Germany and was soon in great demand there as a missionary and a preacher. From her base at Frankfurt am Main she travelled around the country (and also abroad) fighting anti-semitism within the Christian Church. She was one of the first with a vision to prove from the Scriptures that the Jews were not 'rejected' and that God's plan for them was still valid. The veil would one day be taken away from their eyes and they would recognize their Messiah in Jesus. The Church's task is to help them towards this goal, mainly by showing them love, by portraying God for them and by helping to heal the wounds left by past persecution. Mary's books, records and tapes were circulated widely in Germany and God blessed her ministry. Many broken and repentant German people were first set free of the bondage of prejudice and then blossomed out into a deeper and richer understanding of the Gospel by Mary's ministry. Her first visit to us was precious and hearing her preach from the pulpits of English churches was an added bonus. The relationship between Mary and ourselves remained just as strong as it had been before, our year-long separation making little difference. She has been, and is, our most faithful and respected friend with whom we share our concerns and joys, as she does with us.

Turning Points

'I don't want to come to church,' declared Julie one Sunday morning. 'It really doesn't mean anything to me, so why pretend?'

We looked at one another and did not comment. We were not too surprised. Julie had lately become a real little rebel. She refused even to let us kiss her; according to her this was just a stupid habit. Whilst John and Andrew were busily preparing for O and A levels, Julie showed no particular interest in her school subjects or indeed in any other worthwhile activity.

'What will become of our daughter?' we often asked one another. We shared our concern with Mary and she came back with a suggestion. 'Send Julie to a youth camp next summer, away from your influence, into the company of other Christian young people; her horizon might broaden and she might also become more positive towards spiritual matters.' We accepted this advice and next summer Julie went, with her friend Jill, to a Torchbearer camp at Capernwray.

If I go into more detail concerning the events that followed, it is because they had a major effect not only on Julie's life but gradually also on the life of the whole family. This we really did not anticipate when we sent her to the camp in the simple hope that she might become a more serious and more manageable young girl.

Amusing letters arrived from Julie describing her days and how she cunningly escaped the evening Bible studies by hiding behind a thick tree trunk when everybody was called into the assembly room: 'Then I am left alone out there, having a wonderful time, enjoying the silence and the beauty of the evening.' Reading her letters I thought that she was a truly hopeless case and I did not know whether to laugh or cry. We carried on praying. Then came a most surprising letter. I cried when I read it, but this time for joy. George too wiped his eyes surreptitiously as he read.

'Now guess what happened to me last night!' she wrote. 'I was hiding behind my usual tree but this time one of the staff noticed me and made me go in with the others. I did not dare to disobey and resigned myself to endure the occasion. While I was listening to the speaker I had to admit that what he said made sense and I didn't mind any more being made to go to the meeting.'

Here she finished writing, but added another page next day. 'Tonight I went to the Bible study again and this time it was even more interesting. Strangely, it seemed as if all they said was directly addressed to me. How could that be? Nobody knows me here, yet they speak as if they know all about me. Who reveals things to them? At the end there was an appeal for all those who were personally spoken to by God that night to come forward. So was it God who knew all about me and was it he who revealed things to those who spoke to us? Before I knew it I went forward with some others and gave my heart to Jesus.'

'I wonder how seriously we should take this statement?' I said when, after my first feeling of joy, my usual scepticism returned. 'It might be just a passing phase induced by the spiritual atmosphere there.'

George looked at me in some consternation. 'Have you forgotten the fact that this turning point in Julie's life was the very thing we had been praying for?', he asked me, proving with those few words how deeply rooted and real his faith was.

We looked forward eagerly to Julie's return. When she arrived we saw at once that the change in her was beyond all our expectations. We had got back a totally new girl. Her interest now focused on God: that was the main feature of her transformation. She read her Bible regularly and closeted herself in her room for long periods of prayer. Indeed, now we were quite alarmed that she might be overdoing things.

The change was noticeable in many other respects too. She became more interested in her school subjects, devoted more attention to her studies, started to read books and told me one day: 'In the Lord everything makes sense to me suddenly and people have become fascinating too.'

She started to visit my parents regularly in their home – something she had only rarely and reluctantly done in the past. Of course, Shari mama and Dadi were delighted to see her more frequently. It was impossible not to notice the change in her and Dadi remarked one day: 'Well, you know I cannot agree with all you believe but one thing I do know – this girl has become a totally new being since she returned from her holiday.'

Her relationship with the boys changed too. Instead of treating her as a silly little sister, they began to take her more seriously. At school she soon won the confidence of other girls who turned to her with their problems and she became a 'counsellor' to many. She also became very active in the school Christian Union.

Tommy's wedding provided our next milestone. This was the only one of the grandchildren's weddings that my parents were still able to attend together. The young couple started life in a little house in the grounds of a boarding school in Surrey, where Tommy was employed as a physics master.

In 1967 their first child, a little boy, was born. They called him Andrew, after Tommy's father. The birth of 'little Andrew' – as he came to be called in the family – marked yet another milestone for us: he was the first of the fourth generation, the first of Shari mama's and Dadi's great-grandchildren.

John and Andrew began college at the same time. John had spent a year working before being admitted to Nottingham University to read economics (from which he switched to politics one year later) and Andrew went to the University of Edinburgh to study architecture. The house felt empty with only the three of us left, although our frequent visitors made sure that it was not unused. Even so, I could hardly wait for the holidays when the arrival of two lots of trunks indicated the imminent appearance of the boys.

It was strange how the two boys seemed to be on the same wavelength during those college years. Their letters came regularly, often arriving on the very same day. Occasionally they rang home and again they usually phoned on the same evening. If one announced he was coming home for the week-end in term time, without knowing each other's plans the other would come as well. I remember an hilarious incident on one of these occasions. It was in the winter and a heavy snowfall had delayed the train for hours. We sat impatiently at home knowing that both boys were on their way, one from Edinburgh and one from Nottingham. Neither train arrived on schedule. It was long after midnight when the doorbell rang and two laughing bearded faces with snow on their eyelashes and moustaches, peered through the glass door. Not knowing each other's movements, they had caught the last Hertford train at King's Cross, sat in different carriages and only met at our local station where they took the last five minutes walk home together.

More to learn

In 1968 Julie's schooldays came to an end and she went on to Manchester University to do a BA in general arts. After her first academic year, in the summer of 1969, she went for a month to the L'Abri Fellowship in Switzerland.[1] When she came home she could not stop talking about the wonderful place, the beautiful setting high up in the Swiss Alps, the superb view from the chapel and the system under which everyone who came to stay (mainly college students) had to work half a day and study in the other half. She went on to tell us how much she had benefited from the lectures and from the artistic emphasis that underlined all aspects of life there, even the way meals were prepared and served.

'And the organ in the chapel – you have never seen such a lovely thing, designed and made for them specially. We heard it played by real artists. There is also an opera singer living there and when she sings the valleys echo with her gorgeous voice,' Julie enthused. Mostly, however, she spoke of a lady in her early fifties, called Birdie, who individually counselled those in need of her professional experience. 'She is just fantastic, the way she succeeds in getting people to open up to her, and how she makes people recognize what their real problem is and then leads them to the solution. I have learned so much by just observing her. What she does is Christian counselling at its best – and the results are tremendous!' This is how she spoke of Birdie who had obviously made a great impact on her, not only by

---

[1] L'Abri was founded by Dr Francis Schaeffer, an American minister, with the aim of presenting serious answers, biblically valid and intellectually satisfying, to young people searching for God.

her art of counselling but also by her natural and joyful personality. 'She is so normal, loves nice food, is herself a good cook, and loves to read and listen to music in her spare time. She is very spiritual and yet down to earth at the same time' – wrote Julie.

Soon after Julie's return from L'Abri, where she had learned and experienced so much, I lost my temper over something trivial, as I often did. Afterwards, I quickly apologized, as usual. 'I am so sorry, my dear, I really didn't mean it. You know that, don't you? But when I lose my temper I cannot control it. Believe me, I hate it myself and would love to change. I wish I'd inherited Shari mama's lovely nature! She is so balanced and patient, never angry – but I am made differently. What can I do about it?'

'I don't think you can do anything, Mami, but I am sure God can,' was Julie's answer, simple and to the point. 'Have you really asked him to heal your temper? You see Mami, he doesn't only forgive our shortcomings when we feel sincerely sorry for them, he also helps to overcome and conquer them. What we cannot do alone, together with Him we can,' said Julie convincingly. 'One more thing, Mami, coming back to what you said about Shari mama and her lovely nature. Well, I'm not sure this is an advantage for her spiritual growth. For such positive characters the realization of their need of the Lord is more difficult.'

Long after she had returned to college I pondered the meaning of what Julie had said: 'We cannot but God can.' How could that work in reality? Or was it just empty words? Of course I knew that God could change and reform me and to some extent this had been happening throughout the long years of churchgoing which we had already behind us. It is true that God had renewed my thinking and my attitudes – yet there was still so much to leave behind and to grow into! I wondered why God was not quicker in his transformation procedure. Or was there anything in the way? Could it be that I was hindering his work?

When I was impatient with people. and lost my temper,

was my repentance towards them and towards God sincere enough? Or did I just brush the issue aside with a 'Sorry, I didn't mean it,' relying on the forgiveness of those I had hurt? Had I grown at all in this respect since my conversion, and had I changed since the initial stage? And if I now became desperate and wanted to change at all costs, could God 're-mould' me in my advancing age, with my behavioural and thought patterns so fixed by habit? Could he really do it? Was there hope for me?

The next time Julie came home from college – at Christmas 1969 – she mentioned that she had recently been attending the meetings of a small house group in Manchester and had occasionally visited a bigger one in Liverpool too.

'What are they up to?' we asked, with some suspicion. 'Are they some sect? You'd better be careful not to mix yourself up with extreme groups.'

Then she described the groups to us as real worshipping fellowships, rather like big families, the people all knowing one another very well and sharing their joys, sorrows and needs with each other. 'We read the Bible together and rediscover truths that are not really new but neglected for centuries because they were thought to be valid for the time of the apostles only. The way of worshipping is itself unconventional, more like it was in the early church. It is spontaneous, guided by the Holy Spirit, and therefore harmonious and uplifting despite the informality. If they sing a chorus spontaneously, or when members sing together but each to his own tune with his own words, it seems sometimes like an angelic choir.' Her pioneering into news aspects of spiritual life arose in us some doubts: perhaps she was exaggerating and going to extremes? But her college results were good and she had a large circle of friends mainly from the Christian Union, where she had become missionary secretary. Indeed, there was no reason to worry, although our daughter had certainly chosen an unconventional way of life.

It was around this time in 1969 that I started to read more books of a spiritual nature in order to get answers to my continual questions. I picked up a couple of C.S. Lewis' works and found them delightful and helpful. In the Christmas holidays Julie lent me more books, some by Francis Schaeffer and Oswald Chambers, so when I started the year 1970 with a bad attack of flu I had a lot to read in bed. I never suspected what an extended 'leisure time' was in store for me. The flu seemed better and I had been up for a while when one morning I woke with a severe pain in my back and chest. My temperature was very high and when the doctor came he diagnosed an irregularity in my heart-beat. The flu had somehow affected the heart muscles. For a while the doctor visited me twice a day which made us realize that my condition was serious.

Altogether the illness lasted two months and became a most precious period of my life. I spent it mainly by reading and meditating about God and received such peace and rest as I had never felt before. After a while the pains were gone leaving behind a feeling of great weakness. I was unable to write in bed, for example, and it was Dadi who faithfully came every day and acted as my secretary. I dictated letters to him whilst Shari mama took over the household duties. I was really spoilt by all my loved ones but especially by God. His presence was very real in those days and his love overwhelming.

When I was finally permitted to get up the doctor prescribed some tablets that were meant to fortify my heart in the long run. However, their immediate effect was not good and I felt worse. One day during the Easter vacation Julie asked me whether I would let her and George pray for me. I gladly agreed and they laid their hands on me and prayed. It was nice – but there was no difference in my condition. A few days later, when at breakfast I took my usual tablet, Julie looked at me with astonishment, 'Do you still take those, Mami?'

'Well, of course, my dear, the doctor told me to take them.' I replied and she said no more but seemed pensive.

The same afternoon while I was praying, a picture sprang into my mind. I was swimming in very beautiful, transparently clean, turquoise-blue water, then I turned on my back and lay motionless on its surface, absorbed by peace and admiring the beauty of water and sky as they melted together. It was a total abandonment of self, yet I was secure in the knowledge that the water would hold me up. This knowledge was the dominant feature of the vision and crowded out all other thoughts.

I was very joyful whilst kneeling, feeling as if a warm stream was flowing through my whole body. It was a very strange but lovely experience. But what was it God wanted to teach me with the picture and the joy that came with it? Abandonment – yes, that was the key to the message. The explanation came as suddenly as had the picture. I went upstairs, took my tablets and flushed them down the toilet.

Next morning I felt much better and from then on improved every day. On my next appointment with my doctor he was smiling, most satisfied. 'I told you, Mrs Ray, that once your system got used to those tablets your heart would be strengthened and you would feel much better.' I was embarrassed but out of respect for our dear doctor I felt I had to confess to him what I had actually done with the tablets!

Events in 1970

When the Easter vacation was over and the children went back to their colleges, George persuaded me to go to L'Abri where Julie had had such an interesting and blessed time the year before. By then, he too had read some of Dr Schaeffer's books – *Escape from Reason*, and *The God who is There* – and George thought that I could combine a little convalescence with listening to some of the lectures and seeing the place where so many young people came to the Lord. I booked a room in the village (to live in L'Abri itself would have been too tiring) and left for an exciting convalescence. The lectures of Dr Schaeffer were fascinating. I listened to them regularly and also to some of his tapes that we studied in small groups. These were very blessed occasions. We could ask questions when anything was unclear. Listening to Dr Schaeffer personally or on tape I felt that here we had someone with a spirit like John the Baptist, who was preparing the way for some era, some new way of thinking, especially for young people. I could have spent months and months in L'Abri and still cover only a fraction of what Francis Schaeffer had to say, or listen to only a very small part of the taped material piled up in the library. Indeed, I envied the youngsters who often spent a year or even more in those beautiful surroundings, absorbing all the teaching and growing in Biblical knowledge and in the knowledge of God himself. But I knew there must be something more here to transform even those hippy youngsters, arriving with long hair in dirty jeans from all over the world, into serious believers within a few weeks, sometimes even in days.

'What is the secret of these breakthroughs?' I asked Birdie, Julie's great friend, whom I went to see after a few days.

With a mischievous little smile she answered: 'Oh, well, this is the secret: prayer and intercession are going to heaven for every single boy and girl who comes to this place. The most important activity for us staff is to come together and lift these difficult cases up to God. And what you see here is the answer to those prayers.' Then she started to chat about quite different matters in a most natural and casual way. Before I noticed, she knew me inside out!

While I stayed in Huémoz (the tiny Swiss village where L'Abri was) and took part, albeit on a reduced scale, in the activities of L'Abri, I also rested a lot and read. Before I left home I had picked, at random, a book from Julie's bookshelf. It was Agnes Sanford's *The Healing Gifts of the Spirit*. I took it with me on my journey and soon I was totally absorbed in it. The things written there opened a new realm for me. But could it all be true? Is this 'filling' or 'baptism in the Holy Ghost' a reality or only a figurative expression? And if it is an actual event, when does it take place? Does the Holy Ghost – who resides with us after conversion – occupy more and more of our inner being as we open ourselves up to him? Does it depend on our willingness to yield, on our abandonment to God whether and when the 'baptism of the Spirit' takes place?

Abandonment! Here it was again. Was my experience of overwhelming joy, the warmth that flowed through me when in prayer I saw myself floating abandoned on the water, the baptism of the Spirit or a foretaste of it? Or did I have to wait for confirmation and other signs? Did people really pray in tongues, as this book said, or was it humbug, an artificial mumbo-jumbo?

Once again I was full of questions and I could hardly wait to see Julie and share with her what I had read in this book. 'Agnes Sanford says God heals in a miraculous way in answer to prayer. I know this is true but she also says that this is not exceptional; prayer for the sick and the consequent healing ought to be a natural part of the life and practice of every Christian community. Have you heard of this?' I asked her.

'Yes, Mami, and we experienced many such healings in our fellowship in Liverpool. This is why I suggested praying for you and hoped that you would indeed be healed.'

'Now tell me, Julie: do people in your fellowship never go to see a doctor when they are ill – or take medicine? I think that this would be taking things too far.'

'It certainly would be, I agree with you, Mami. God heals in various ways: in the miraculous way by his touch, as he did in your case, or through medical advice and prescribed medicine. One cannot and should not put down strict rules – God's ways are higher than ours. On each occasion one should pray first for healing and then be guided as to whether or not medical advice is still necessary.'

'And have you ever heard of praying and singing in tongues?' I carried on, bombarding her with my questions.

'Oh yes, you remember me telling you about the beautiful, unconducted yet harmonious singing in the fellowship? Well, people sing not only to their own tunes with their own words but also in their own tongues.'

I was more and more amazed. 'Now one more question, Julie: do you yourself pray or sing in tongues?'

'Yes, I do.'

'But you kept it all a secret for such a long while! You never told us a word about it.'

'But, Mami, you would have taken me to a psychiatrist,' Julie answered and we both burst out laughing! How well she had understood our attitudes and reactions.

I became very interested in what I had read, and what Julie had confirmed, and it was my wish to see, judge and also test what was true in all these matters. 'If only I could attend such a gathering,' I said to Julie. But she did not know any in London and we had, therefore, to put the whole matter aside for the time being.

In the meantime both George and I experienced a growing desire to extend our knowledge and understanding of God, partly for our own benefit and partly also for the sake of the church members in our road group. This road group system had been introduced a short while previously, before Keith, our minister, had left the church to take up another appointment. He had entrusted George and myself with the leadership of one of the groups although we had felt that neither our knowledge nor our experience was broad enough for such a task. Similarly, during the long years of interregnum following Keith's departure, we had felt that our spiritual appetites were left unsatisfied by the church. Then, later that summer, Julie heard of a small group of people meeting in a house only a few minutes drive away from us. We got in touch with their leader and he invited me to join them one Saturday evening. I accepted the invitation and sat through a most unusual meeting where people were displaying an embarrassingly emotional love towards God that I found disturbing, even off-putting. At the end, one of the group asked me whether I had been blessed by the meeting. I could not restrain my disappointment and burst out: 'Blessed? I am sorry – not at all. It seemed to me group therapy rather than worship.' With these words I wanted to escape as quickly as possible but at the car the same man caught me again.

'Don't make a hasty decision, give it another chance.' His appeal suddenly brought to mind Mary's words after my first attendance at Bible study many years ago in Hungary. Then I had been bewildered and repulsed by prayers said aloud and had been disinclined to take part in such meetings again. But Mary had insisted that I give it another chance . . .

A few days later I went for a private chat with John, the leader of that small group. He spoke of much that appeared to me sound and true and let me listen to a recording of a large fellowship which included the singing of choruses and singing 'in tongues'. Even on tape it was lovely and I could not deny the sincerity of the praise and joy that I heard: doubtless there was real life in it.

From then on I attended the meetings at John's place from time to time and later more regularly. George came with me once and at first reacted exactly as I had but then he also acknowledged that if we really wanted to grow spiritually and know more about God, this fellowship certainly had something to offer.

It was during that same summer that our son John graduated, after which he applied for a place with the Voluntary Service Overseas (VSO) and was accepted for a teaching post in Ceylon (now Sri Lanka). His teaching year would start at Christmas. We approved of this venture and felt it was right, although dreading, of course, the year when he would be so far away.

Andrew had just finished his practical year, the fourth year of his architectural studies, which he had spent in Germany. Having bought himself a used car with his savings, he decided to drive home via Switzerland and stop for two weeks at this famous L'Abri place that Julie and I were so impressed with. John joined him there from England.

For our two boys the stay at L'Abri became very significant indeed. John and Andrew had never rebelled against churchgoing as Julie had before her conversion, but their belief had been very superficial. During their holiday at L'Abri, however, Christianity became a personal conviction and the basis for their future lives. Since then their steady spiritual growth has been established.

This holiday was to become very memorable for another reason also for it was there that Andrew met Peggie, an American girl attending college in the States from where she too had come to 'this famous L'Abri place'. Her father was a missionary doctor and the family had spent a very long time in Iran, where Peggie had been brought up. Like our sons, she was well acquainted with Christianity, yet there was a need for a personal decision. This is why she had come to L'Abri, two weeks before her meeting with Andrew. The two of them fell in love and she returned to the States via London. For a few days she stayed in our house and we saw that theirs was a serious attachment. They certainly made a very handsome pair.

'Are you a smoker, Mr Leimdorfer,' asked the lung specialist, fumbling with his papers.

'Not now, but in my youth I was a chain-smoker,' admitted Dadi. There seemed to be a long pause before the consultant spoke again. We sat silently in his surgery waiting for his verdict on Dadi's condition. Four months earlier he had started coughing and one day had lost his voice altogether. It was obviously something more than laryngitis. Our family doctor had sent him for X-rays followed by a bronchoscopy, the result of which we were now awaiting. The consultant looked up from his files and spoke in a grave yet gentle manner: 'We could give you some radium treatment, Mr Leimdorfer, but I believe it would cause nausea and I do not want you to feel even more ill. It would not bring about any dramatic improvement in your condition either. So let us leave things to run their course. Do you understand me, Mr Leimdorfer?' Dadi was pale and only nodded, but by the time we reached home he had brushed aside the verdict on his condition and had decided to carry on living as normally as he was able; we all hoped and prayed that a miracle would heal him, or at least that he would be spared great suffering. By autumn his cough had become more intense, but he never complained and only took the occasional paracetamol to ease his pain.

Births and deaths – arrivals and departures

By this time Tommy and his family were living in Ashford (Middlesex) where Tommy was head of the grammar school's science department. When they moved there, after having been quite a few years at the King Edward Boarding School, they had been in need of a house. Once again the Lord showed his providential care. This time Dadi was notified of the success of his claim for compensation from the German government for losses during the Nazi era. It came most opportunely and the amount was just enough to use as a deposit on Tommy's house. This house was relatively near and Shari mama and Dadi used to visit them regularly. Little Andrew was a great friend to them and, although I remember him as a boisterous little chap, he was very gentle, caring and courteous with Shari mama and Dadi when they visited the house.

In November a little girl was born to Valerie and

Tommy. Dadi was still able to go with Shari mama and see Gillie when she was only a few days old. Apart from the thrill that goes with such events, Gillie's birth will always remain particularly memorable for me. I was meant to stay with them for a few days to help after the baby was born. As soon as Tommy rang to say that Valerie's labour had begun, I went to their house. This was in the morning and I expected to find a baby by the time I arrived. However, the midwife told me that the labour was not progressing well and there might be a delay of many hours. She also hinted at a slight complication that alarmed me. While Tommy and the midwife were upstairs in Valerie's bedroom I started to pray in the kitchen. I was more and more encouraged to pray, then to praise with hymns and choruses, as if the vigorous melodies would hasten the baby's progress in breaking through the obstacle, whatever it was, to his or her arrival. My anxiety gradually left me and then it seemed to me that I 'heard', although soundlessly, that the child was to be born at a quarter to two. It was half past twelve on my watch. I quickly made some lunch for the midwife and asked her to come down to eat. 'You'd better hurry a little,' I told her when she took her time over the pudding, 'the baby will come soon.' She gave me a scathing look, obviously considering me to be meddling in affairs beyond my comprehension. However, a few minutes after one o'clock Tommy, who had remained upstairs with his wife, rushed in. 'Please come,' he said to the midwife, 'there is a change; it might have started again.'

I was not a bit surprised. Yet when the cuckoo clock struck a quarter to two and I heard the first cry of the baby I burst into tears. 'Thank you, Lord, for this new life and also for revealing secrets to such an unworthy person as me.' It was a tremendous joy, a tremendous experience.

Christmas came and with it the departure of John for Ceylon. He left his overcoat with us as he boarded the plane for a warmer climate. I wished I could skip the coming year, to his return after the twelve long months, and could put the same coat back on to his shoulders again.

Andrew had spent Christmas with Peggie and her family in Philadelphia in order to come to some definite conclusion about their future plans. With remarkable zeal – typical of Andrew, once he had made up his mind – he sold his VW beetle and bought himself a return ticket to the United States. So a couple of days after John's departure we went to the airport again, this time to wait in the arrivals lounge for Andrew to turn up. After the hugs and kisses Andrew said matter-of-factly, 'Peggie and I are now engaged.'

They planned their wedding for August 1972, straight after their respective graduations. There would be yet another year and a half of separation, yet they hoped to meet once or twice in the interim and the time would pass quickly with all their studies to be completed.

In January 1971 Dadi became very weak. Even so, they still made the short distance from their flat to our house every day but it took him gradually longer and longer. Leaning on his stick, Dadi would stop frequently and by the time he arrived he would be exhausted. He usually fell asleep in an armchair for a little while before attempting to return home, always refusing a lift in the car. He wanted to prove himself capable of at least this little exercise. On one of the last such occasions, when he woke up from his short sleep, he looked at me and said very emphatically: 'Thank you, thank you.' I never knew what he meant, yet I am sure it was something important to him. Perhaps I may be permitted to guess that secretly he had accepted in his heart something of what we had tried, often rather clumsily, to convey to him about the love of God. Maybe he wanted to give a sign of appreciation for my seemingly fruitless efforts.

He stayed in bed for just three days. The last night I tried to make Shari mama rest, at least for a few hours, while I kept vigil in their bedroom. 'The little lamp can be turned up to give more effective light if you want to read,' Dadi whispered to me from his bed, showing his concern for me even in those last few hours of his life. Then he seemed to be resting quite well and while I watched him a joy overcame me that was quite unnatural considering the situation. Here was my father, dying, and I was comforted, reassured as if held in God's arms. But what about Dadi? Lord, does he know you? What will happen when he meets you face to face? Somehow the uncertainty over his salvation disappeared. There was no explanation – only a reassurance.

When Shari mama replaced me in the middle of the night I went home. A couple of hours later the telephone rang: we should come at once. By the time we arrived it was all over. There was only Shari mama, bewildered and silently weeping. We spent the night there together until the doctor came to confirm the death. Then we took Shari mama home with us. We knew she would live with us from that morning onward and our house would become her home once again.

The widowed Shari mama

Dadi's funeral service in the crematorium was simple and very moving. The rabbi we contacted was very understanding; what he said – and what we sang – was all selected in such a way that nobody present was made to feel at all awkward: it could have been a Jewish, as well as a Christian, funeral. But the most significant and really symbolic aspect lay in the fact that when we arrived at the chapel and the coffin was carried through the open doors, we found to our surprise that the rabbi was standing by one doorpost and our minister by the other. They had obviously arranged this between themselves and it showed real insight and understanding on their part.

In her grief Shari mama was just as remarkable as she had always been. She let herself be persuaded to take a little tranquillizer for the first few nights, then she stopped them altogether. She was often sleepless for hours, as she admitted in the mornings, but she spent those hours 'remembering'. She called to mind one episode after another of her life with Dadi, reliving all their joys and sorrows, again and again. In this way she worked through her grief and found comfort in her bereavement.

She also insisted on carrying on a normal way of life during the day and this helped her to keep a balance and not to be overwhelmed by grief. She had breakfast in bed, read her Bible and had her prayer time. She got up in the late morning and was soon down in the kitchen, asking for a job to do. She usually helped with preparing meals and loved to do those time-consuming little extras for which I had no patience. When visitors came, she was in her element: she made exquisite sandwiches, decorated the table, arranged the flowers and folded the napkins into unusual shapes. She was also the one who took out, with long tweezers, the remnants of feathers from the inadequately plucked turkey or chicken! I can still see her doing this very boring and uninteresting work with the same patience as for any other, more satisfying job.

After lunch she would retire to her room to read on her bed and to have a short sleep. In the afternoons and evenings again she would help in whatever way she could and then would settle down in front of her television and watch the news and anything else worth seeing. She imposed this discipline on herself to keep alive her interest in all matters of politics and world events. As she said: that was a medicine to prevent her from self-pity and from becoming inward-looking.

Once or twice, when I entered her room unexpectedly, I caught her silently weeping but she immediately wiped her tears and practically apologized for her weakness. She was strong yet soft, sweet and wise throughout those weeks, and also during the later years of her widowhood.

We installed Shari mama in two rooms of our house, by

moving the boys over to her flat. This was arranged very quickly so that she was surrounded by her own furniture, making her feel more at home in our house. But because the boys were away in college the flat was empty for weeks so she went over regularly, mainly to water the beautiful indoor lime that we were unable to move because of its size. We knew though, that it was like a pilgrimage for her, back to the place where she had spent such peaceful years together with Dadi.

A new chapter in Shari mama's spiritual life was beginning. She now joined us regularly at all occasions of worship, something which she had not done before because it would have meant leaving Dadi alone at home. By restraining herself in this way she had managed to avoid the inevitable rift that is so often apparent between married couples of uneven measures of faith. Instead of treading a separate path, she had adapted herself to the situation and through her patient love had achieved, I am sure, some response in Dadi, perhaps more than his pride would have allowed him to show. Thus the mission of the submissive wife had been accomplished.

She now became a faithful member of the fellowship, never missing a meeting, as if to make up for the years she had had to be without the company of other believers. For her – just as for us – the hours we spent in company delving further into God's character and purpose towards ourselves opened up new depths and new heights.

The fellowship itself had been expanding since our first attendance. The term 'house group' was no longer appropriate for a gathering that now required premises capable of seating thirty or forty (and sometimes many more) people and new people were still joining.

One Saturday a sweet looking young girl came for the first time with her mother, who was a regular member of the group, to observe our meeting at first hand. Ros was a young doctor, a little worried about her mother 'mixing herself' up with this 'extreme' group of Christians. She turned up repeatedly until finally she too became a regular and a most faithful member of the fellowship. When one day I heard of a vacancy occurring in our local surgery I mentioned it to Ros; she applied for the job, got it, and thus became our GP. It was wonderful to have her as our doctor and she became a real blessing to the entire practice and also to the fellowship. For our family she has become, above all, a most precious friend.

Indian summer

The warm gentle glow of October sunshine embraces the quaint little resort of Balatonfüred. The period houses of the previous century contribute to the atmosphere of the 'good old days', reminding one that this resort has been a favourite holiday place for generations. The lakeshore is lined with old trees that are at present decked with the rust and gold of autumn. In contrast, the water is coloured the palest, most luminous blue and is as calm as a mirror. The noisy summer crowd has gone leaving nothing but peace and beauty, the most perfect setting for rest and relaxation, especially for elderly people.

This was exactly what Shari mama, her brother Pali and his wife were able to enjoy that happy week together at Balatonfüred, before her eightieth birthday. We had wondered how best to celebrate the great day without causing Shari mama undue sorrow, this being her first birthday without Dadi, and the idea of the journey had gradually taken shape. George suggested that she might like to spend a few weeks in Hungary again, seeing her brother Pali and his wife Liszka, who were the only ones of her generation still alive, and also seeing all her nieces and the other members of her family. To celebrate her birthday in the midst of them and in the country where she had spent most of her life seemed a good idea. George generously accepted my absence for three weeks so that I could escort

Shari mama on this trip, the first part of which was to be spent at the lake.

Every morning we went for a walk with Pali and Liszka. It was a slow walk with Shari mama using her stick and Uncle Pali, who once was so tall and erect, now treading slowly at her side with his head still high, yet somehow looking very frail. I could not help feeling that this might be their last meeting together. Each day at mid-morning we went to a lakeside cafeteria and sat on the open terrace, looking out over the velvety, sunlit water, talking of long-gone years, of which their memories were as heart-warming as the sweet autumn sunshine.

While these three had their coffee and chat I was off on my solitary walks on the hills high above the lake and there my thoughts returned to England. To be away for a length of time from Britain and to become again part of the Hungarian set-up produced a strange sensation. Where was my home? Was it here where I was brought up? Though I had been uprooted from here I still felt a sense of belonging. But my real home was in England where my family and my house were awaiting my return. In a way I belonged to both countries – and in another sense to neither. Oddly enough, this discovery filled me with joy. What liberty I had, what exceptional grace of God not to be bound by traditions, by one's background or by any other ties that pin one down firmly to this earth. 'I am free, Lord, I am free!' I felt light enough for my feet to leave the ground, as if I could take off and fly straight into the blue horizon where sky and water meet in glorious light.

The celebration of Shari mama's birthday took place in the private room of a Budapest restaurant. She was showered with many gifts but what was more important to her was the love she received from all present at the occasion.

Our stay in Hungary had come to an end. We sat silently in the plane, recollecting some of the heartwarming details of our visit. Beneath us the continent slipped from view and soon the contours of the English shore would be visible.

The stewardess offered coffee or tea. 'Tea, please' we both said eagerly, and it was the first really good cup of tea we had had for three weeks.

There was a real sense of homecoming.

About weddings

1972 turned out to be a year of weddings. Andrew and Peggie decided to get married in Edinburgh, and on that occasion we met many old friends who came to attend the wedding. We were also able to get to know Peggie's family, who stopped off in Edinburgh on their way from America to Afghanistan where Peggie's father was to take up a new appointment in a mission hospital. His moving address to the young couple was the highlight of their church wedding.

The venue for the celebrations was a beautiful Scottish mansion a few miles from Edinburgh that we had found by chance when we started to organize the wedding. The owner and his wife let us have their home for a few days and there were just enough bedrooms to put up all the wedding guests. Between the meals that were served to us in the elegant dining room we enjoyed sitting on the paved terrace of the house, overlooking the park and the fields belonging to the estate. God provided such a princely setting for the occasion (costing less than a stay in an ordinary guest house). It was a luxury none of us could ever have afforded.

Of course, Shari mama took part in all this fun and wedding preparation. When at last we sat in the pew of the church I glanced at her. She was smartly dressed in her pale lilac two-piece, with matching light flowery blouse, a pale lilac straw hat and a small fur around her shoulder to complete the outfit. She looked what indeed she was, a real lady.

Barbara, John's girl friend, came to the wedding,

although she nearly had to cancel because of an unexpected operation. However, although still weak, she managed to make the journey up to Edinburgh. The operation had revealed that she had a large number of fibroids that might prevent her ever becoming pregnant. The diagnosis caused her great sorrow and she was on the point of giving up their growing friendship, not wishing to tie John to a marriage that might not yield a family. But John had become even more determined to marry Barbara and face with her whatever the future might hold for them.

At that time Barbara was not a believer and John was very keen for her to find the way that he himself had discovered during the last couple of years. Birdie, the family's great friend from L'Abri, who was among the wedding guests, summed up the situation and invited Barbara for a 'convalescence' in her cottage in Huémoz, Switzerland. Barbara accepted gladly. John accompanied her there and left her in Birdie's capable hands and loving care.

When Barbara arrived home a month later I could hardly believe my eyes. The change in her was remarkable: her eyes shone and on her face there was no longer any trace of sorrow. I did not have to ask any questions, it was so clearly written on her face that she had become one whom the Lord comforted, one who knew her Saviour. They fixed their wedding for Christmas. So we could look forward to a second happy event in the same year.

After their honeymoon, Andrew and Peggie installed themselves in Shari mama's flat. (John offered to move out, into rented accommodation.) Thus, this flat started to fulfil its third purpose: first it had been the home of my parents, then of my two sons, and now that of Andrew and Peggie.

The wedding of John and Barbara took place on 29 December. It was a gloriously sunny day, quite unusually warm for the season. Barbara did not have to shiver in her cream crêpe wedding dress. It was a lovely ceremony in a Church of England church in Manchester where her parents lived, followed by a reception with a gorgeous buffet. Barbara's parents had already met Shari mama, whom they quickly grew to love and to whom they were exceptionally kind on the wedding day. This time Mary Hajos was also among the guests–John's real fairy godmother who held him, and from now on Barbara too, in the Lord's presence by her faithful daily prayers.

Journey to Israel

We planned to visit Israel in March 1973. George was keen to see his cousins again after so many years and to meet their families. (The younger one joined his brother in Israel after having finished school.)

We started to prepare ourselves well in advance by reading books about Israel for we had to admit that we had not followed the recent history of this country with the interest it deserved from all who wanted to understand God's plans for his people.

Now, on reading various exciting reports and publications from several sources, an entirely novel theological insight presented itself for us concerning the mysterious rebirth of the state of Israel.

Well-known passages now took on a new meaning as we re-read them. Like Ezekiel's book, chapter 11, verses 16 and 17:

> 'Thus says the Lord: Though I removed them (the Jews) far off among the nations, and though I scattered them among the countries, yet I have been a sanctuary to them for a while in the countries where they have gone . . . I will gather you from the peoples and assemble you out of the countries where you have been scattered, and I will give you the land of Israel.'

A very firm promise, no doubt. But was this promise referring to our present time? Has Israel any further part to play in God's plans as a nation? Another prophet gives the answer. Jeremiah's ministry preceded that of Ezekiel by just a few years and to him it was announced that:

> 'The Lord, who gives the sun for light by day and the fixed order of the moon and the stars for light by night . . .
> If this fixed order departs . . . then shall the descendants of Israel cease from being a nation before me for ever' (Jeremiah chapter 31 verses 35-36).

Well, the system of the sun and the moon is still with us, so the promise still stands. Moreover, we can read it somewhat later in Ezekiel, in more concrete form:

> 'I will take you from the nations and gather you from all the countries and bring you into your own land' (Ezekiel chapter 36 verse 24).
>
> 'You shall dwell in the land which I gave to your fathers' (verse 28).
>
> But not only the land: 'A new heart I will give you and a new spirit I will put within you' (verse 26).
>
> Then there is the best known prophecy about the valley of dry bones that gradually come back to life (Ezekiel chapter 37).

All these passages suddenly began to make sense; they – and the historical events that have surrounded the rebirth of the state of Israel – provide the evidence that it is indeed God who gathers up the Jewish people into their original homeland; it is with his help that the desert becomes fertile again and in the place of ruins bustling new towns spring up. No doubt the work is being carried out by human hands but it follows God's blueprint. He puts down the groundwork that makes the fulfilment of his plan possible – the plan he disclosed through his prophets concerning a Messianic age, when Israel is supposed to serve the Lord as a nation and not as a scattered people.

How was it that we had totally ignored these parts of the Scriptures before? It was certainly not because we had become Christians. In fact, we first studied the Old Testament in depth at the time of our conversion and had continued this practice. As a result we understood Judaism better than before. Yet, although we were thrilled by the thought that many persecuted Jews had found relative peace and rest in the land of Israel, the theological significance and impact of the historical birth of the State of Israel had not come home to us. We wondered why this revelation had been hidden so long. But now that we had finally discovered the tremendous significance of the fulfilment of the prophecies in our lifetime we became more and more excited at the prospect of experiencing personally the miraculous development of this land.

We left London in the middle of March and stayed in Israel about three weeks. The journey surpassed all our expectations. Every day brought new impressions to reinforce our belief that something tremendous was happening in the land. This we felt despite the various – and numerous – negative features which we also could not help but see. Yet, among agnostic Zionists as well as among fanatical Jewish believers, in this land of diverse peoples from all parts of the world, God is at work. Some really positive features of ordinary everyday life provide evidence for this. But we believe that the outpouring of the Spirit that will restore the nation spiritually still remains a promise for the future.

When we returned from Israel we invited relatives and friends round to share our experiences with them. Shari mama was the one who enjoyed our reports and slides most. Not so some of our other guests, for whom this subject was totally new. They thought that our fascination with it and the significance we attached to Israel as a country and as a nation sprang from the fact that we were Jewish and therefore felt sympathetic towards Jews in general. To them the destiny of Israel did not mean more than that of any other nation: God loves all men equally and makes those who are in his will prosper whether Jew or Gentile, Israeli or English. In their view the prophecies were given to the Church and are valid in a spiritual context rather than as an historical reality. But we remained convinced that with the passing of time history will prove that the prophecies in the Scriptures refer indeed to both: the church – the spiritual Israel – and Israel as the nation of the Jews.

A burial place

Summer 1973 saw us back in Edinburgh once more. Because of an accumulation of leave days George was taking an extended vacation and we wondered where to spend these three precious months of free time. What better location could we find than somewhere near Julie whom we saw so seldom?

Julie had spent the last year in Auchen Heath, a Scottish village. After finishing her postgraduate studies in Edinburgh, which qualified her for youth and community work, she joined the staff of the house belonging to Dr and Mrs Kelly. She wanted to savour the life of the little community that had sprung up in what was originally the private residence of the Kellys. The few months she had originally planned to spend at Auchen Heath House had by now been repeatedly extended and there was no prospect of her coming back to London. So we agreed that she should find some accommodation for us – and for Shari mama – not too far from Auchen Heath House.

In Edinburgh, Julie met us at the station and drove in front to show us the way through the city and afterwards through the lovely Scottish countryside. We were eager to see the place that was to be our home for the next three months. 'It is a very simple shepherd's cottage built on farmland, away from the so-called civilized world,' she had said in her letter. That would suit us fine for the summer.

As it turned out, the shepherd's cottage was only big enough for two; however, in nearby Biggar we found a friendly lady who let a room to Shari mama and was willing to cater for her, so we were able to look forward to a good rest with frequent walks and pleasant drives, and of course a lot of time spent with Julie, whenever she was free.

Well, things did not turn out quite as expected. God's hand was very much in evidence during this long holiday but it very soon became obvious that he had some other thoughts of how we ought to use it. Thinking back, it is clear that Auchen Heath was to become a perfect tool in God's hand for breaking down a good deal of the pride that still existed in us. The devotion of the couple who owned that grand place, Jack and Eileen, their total dedication of themselves, their house and their income to people in need, was all new to us. In the mirror of their lives ours seemed totally egotistic and carnal.

The close observation of the Kellys' lives had a greater influence on George than any words. Here was a couple – Jack, a respected consultant of an important hospital and Eileen, gracious and charming – owning this beautiful mansion and the vast grounds around it. And instead of keeping it to themselves, they had opened it up to people in various states of distress: alcoholics, victims of broken marriages, hippies who had lost any aim in life, and so on. They themselves occupied only one room apart from their bedroom and rooms for their children. The rest of the enormous house – the other bedrooms, the library, the spacious lounge and the dining room – were all at the disposal of those who were their 'guests' and the workers who helped to run the place. Eileen herself was on her feet all day running the big household and she was also the one who would sit up at night with anyone who needed comfort or just the presence of a caring person. Jack came home from his hospital work and spent all his free time either with people needing the benefit of his wisdom, or studying the scriptures in preparation for his next sermon.

I am sure that the impact of Jack's and Eileen's personalities awakened something in us that would prepare us for events to come: it was no coincidence that we were able to spend these three months near Auchen Heath.

We also regularly attended the services held in the big lounge of the house. It was there we understood fully the concepts of 'dying to oneself' and 'living unto God', concepts which we saw here practised as well as preached.

It was also a rather stirring experience to see our daughter's way of life at close hand. We knew that Julie helped with any kind of job because everybody in the house shared all the tasks equally. Yet to hear or read something in a letter and to see it actually happen are two very different things. Here was our dear and precious daughter, who had obtained a degree and an extra diploma, now peeling potatoes, cleaning the house, making beds and washing up! Sometimes she helped in the garden and, of course, she also helped with counselling, but mostly she worked as a domestic. This way of life was her own choice; she gave up career prospects, income and the best years of her youth. She wasn't going out with anybody, had no opportunity for travelling, no cultural life, in fact had only physical work and spiritual activity.

We did not have much time or opportunity to be with Julie because she was so busy with the house. Nevertheless, in the few good conversations we had I once asked: 'Tell me Julie, are you not overdoing this 'dying to yourself' a bit? You may become colourless, uninteresting and less attractive not only as a woman but also as a personality. One ought to be at one's best in order to be a good advertisement for God. I don't think a 'dead' disciple or missionary can be really effective.'

'Don't worry about me, Mami,' was her reassuring reply. 'This state of death is only temporary while God deals with certain aspects of my character. One day there will be a 'resurrection'. Then all that you mean by colour, the creative interests and the initiatives that are temporarily faded, will be restored, I hope.' Then she added with a sheepish smile: 'Who knows, I might even become an improvement on the original!'

In this way she repeatedly tried to reassure us, expressing her certainty that this place was right for her at present and that she was merely following God's will in the manner in which she lived. She also pointed out that she was meeting so many types of problem cases in Auchen Heath House that being there provided the best possible training for her, even in professional terms, at that point of time.

This sounded convincing enough, yet it was not something we could accept easily. All the pride we had accumulated during our upbringing had to be thrown away and this was a painful process. I began to think that our Scottish holiday cottage provided a lovely and comfortable 'burial place' for many features of our 'old selves' which needed to be dealt with.

Shari mama came with us nearly everywhere and was greatly impressed. She did not say much but her interest in spiritual matters grew and deepened during this period. We visited a few lovely places when the weather permitted but it was an exceptionally rough summer in Scotland with wind, rain, mist, fog and only occasional sunshine. Maybe in better weather we would have enjoyed more outings but spent certainly less time on reading and concentrating on what God had to show us.

More about healing

Peggie was pregnant, expecting her baby in December while Barbara grieved at the lack of any sign of pregnancy. In fact Barbara had a lot of pain, indicating that despite her recent operation she was not really well. She knitted for Peggie's baby and often shed hidden tears on the matinée jacket she was making. This was the family situation when we returned from our Scottish holiday.

The same autumn (1973) Ian Andrews came to our

fellowship in Southgate and stayed for a whole week. He taught us about the healing power of the Spirit and how God releases it when we pray to him either for ourselves or for others.

I asked Barbara to take part in these meetings and she and John came together. After the first few evenings Ian was praying for those who had asked him to. Barbara was not among them. She looked at me with shining eyes and said: 'I am not asking for prayer, I *know* I am already healed.' There was such conviction in her voice that Ros, who sat near me and who was also Barbara's doctor, looked at me with an encouraging smile. Quickly counting on my fingers I whispered into Ros's ear: 'If this is so she will have a baby in August or September.'

At the same meeting Ian prayed for George, after giving out words of knowledge about someone present suffering from regular backaches. George did not recognise this was for him, taking the view that his was not a sickness but a permanent condition; yet because Ian insisted he finally asked for prayer. It was short and simple. I remember that George took out a handkerchief from his pocket and wiped beads of sweat from his face and forehead. He said it was a strange experience but apart from heat he had not felt anything. However, next morning he woke up without any trace of his usual pain, something that had not happened before, despite his regular visits to Bath for physiotherapy and other treatment. So this painless morning was a surprise. 'It might be just a coincidence,' he thought; but next day, and the day after, there was still no pain. For six months, all symptoms left him. Later on they occasionally returned but in a much milder form which could be checked by a hot shower or a brisk walk. He has needed no further treatment since.

The Lord provides

Danny was born on 6 December to Peggy and Andrew, giving tremendous happiness to the whole family. How absorbed one can become with one's first grandchild! With what excitement we followed every new phase of babyhood, and indeed of the first years!

Soon after this happy event, Andrew rang us one Saturday morning. Could he and Peggie come and see us about something that concerned their fellowship and themselves? They sounded quite excited. While I prepared the coffee cups in anticipation of a good chat I could not help smiling about the very special situation our family was in. Here we were, all believing Christians, yet belonging to different worshipping bodies. John and Barbara, after settling down, had joined a lively Free Evangelical Church near their home and John had come to be elected a deacon there. Andrew and Peggie had joined a fellowship functioning along lines similar to ours but the membership consisted more of young people, either couples with little children or single people. Andrew became an elder there. Julie worshipped and worked with the fellowship of Auchen Heath and Tommy and Valerie had recently joined the Society of Friends.

Sometimes I am quite sad not to have my family around me on Sunday mornings. I would love to worship together with them – but this apparently is not to be our lot. However, when, on rare occasions, it happens, it is an extra treat. Is this situation coincidental or is there a reason for it? Could it be an extra privilege to be connected, through our children, to various other worshipping bodies so that we can hear their news, follow their churches' development and learn from one another by sharing our experiences?

I was looking forward to hearing the latest news from Andrew and Peggie's fellowship. What they came to tell us was that the house next to that of Ken, the leader of their fellowship, had come on to the market. The fellowship would love to see this property occupied by one of its members, and possibly have a meeting room there on the ground floor, since Ken's sitting room had recently become too small. Could they, Andrew and Peggie, be the ones to purchase this house? They asked for our advice and opinions. We agreed that this was a very serious proposition and could only be undertaken by a joint effort from the whole family. We promised to think and pray about it separately and then meet again and see what could be done.

John and Barbara were involved in the 'thinking' as well as Julie who happened to be at home for a short holiday. Soon Tommy and family arrived for their usual after-Christmas stay with us and we all came together one night to discuss the issue. How could matters be arranged so as to accord with God's will – if it was his plan to purchase the house?

First, we agreed that this venture might well represent yet a new challenge from God. The question was how to respond to it. George spoke first: 'The savings I have I gladly give and if I can obtain a loan from my bank that too would be at your disposal.'

'No need to ask for a loan,' said Shari mama, 'Andrew and Peggie won't be using my flat any more, neither will I need an extra home ever again. As you all know the original buyer of the flat was Tommy but later Dadi helped him to purchase his own house. In consequence this flat is mine and I can do what I like with it so I pass it on to my grandchildren. Take your inheritance now. It should, therefore, be your joint decision whether you keep it or sell it and if you do decide to sell, whether to use the money to enable Andrew to buy this house.'

'Well, for our part we would willingly give our share to Andrew,' was John's immediate reaction. 'Though we trust that one day we will have a family, for the time being there is no trace of it. For the two of us our present rented accommodation is acceptable and we are not thinking further ahead.' Barbara nodded in agreement. (At that time she did not suspect how imminent her pregnancy was.)

'As for me,' said Julie, 'being a single girl I am in no need of a large amount of money. And in any case I want to learn what it is to live 'by faith', trusting God for everything. I am sure that if I ever need a home God will provide it, as he provides my daily needs now.'

Tommy listened and smiled mysteriously, as if he had a mischievous thought in his mind. 'If all of you agree to sell the flat I will too, but since it is still in my name I should be permitted to make a condition: I want to specify who the buyer should be,' he said.

'Come on, tell us what you have in mind,' said one of us.

'Hear, hear, what have you got up your sleeve?' we asked, all agog to hear his answer.

'Well, my condition is that the buyer should be John.' We looked at him surprised and none of us understood what he meant. He then explained: 'John will buy the flat from me, as it is in my name, and the mortgage he obtains could go towards Andrew's house. I don't want my share either for the time being, having a home already. It is John who may need one next, even if at present he seems satisfied with what he has got.' It sounded wise, we laughed happily, in total agreement.

I was delighted with the way the subject had been handled; with co-operation, love for one another, and a zeal for God – the right basis for a right solution.

We all went to inspect the house in question. Shari mama slowly climbed the many stairs up to the very top, to the attic, then slowly down again. 'Well, if you want my opinion, this house would be a very difficult place to live in because of all those steps and different levels; and it is not good value as an investment because of its size. Its price will not go up in line with that of other houses.' It was a sober evaluation and our enthusiasm seemed to wane as fast as it had come.

I will never forget the next morning. I woke early from sleep and as if from deep within me the Lord asked me: 'If it had been an excellent property, a really good investment, would you have decided to buy the house?' I felt uneasy and the answer came to me clearly. If this whole project was for the Lord's sake, did it matter that it was not a comfortable house and not a good investment? I became really excited and could hardly wait until the usual morning routine was over; then, without telling anyone I went upstairs to the study and prayed that if this inner voice was from God it should be confirmed by some other sign. I opened the Bible at random and asked God to answer me from His own word; my eyes fell on 1 Chronicles chapter 22. In that chapter King David commissions his son Solomon to build a house for the Lord, a house that he had himself wanted to build but could not because his life was not spotless enough; the task therefore had been given to his son, although David would give him all possible help and the benefit of his experience.

It was stunning, so clear and unmistakeable was the message. No other passage in the whole Bible would have been more relevant to the subject. I took my Bible and my coat and rushed over to Peggie to show her the passage. We agreed that it was clear guidance on the issue and she accepted her part of the deal: the very tiring house. So often since, when I am there and see how many times she and Andrew have to rush up and down to answer telephone calls, or the doorbell, I hear Shari mama's voice and her correct judgement. Yet all of us know, and even Shari mama was given the time to witness it, that this house has indeed become a 'house of God', a worshipping place for an ever increasing fellowship. The huge meeting room downstairs was soon outgrown and the wall between it and the lounge removed to accommodate all the members who meet regularly in Andrew's house for worship, meals or social occasions.

I often think of the acquisition of the house and all the events that led up to it. I am still amazed at the timing of it, just after our stay at Auchen Heath, where we were shown the use and importance of such a place, after the miracles of healing we had experienced, and after the birth of our first grandchild. Our year was indeed crowned by the Lord enabling us as a family to 'build a house' for his worship.

When John and Barbara moved into Shari mama's flat, Barbara was already expecting their baby. It was a stormy pregnancy, often touch-and-go whether Barbara would be able to keep the child. Ros had to rush over quite a few times with injections yet Barbara never doubted that this child was God's gift and that it would be born all right. A very complicated birth was anticipated but it turned out to be a smooth and easy one. Mattie was the prettiest newborn baby I have ever seen. 'No wonder,' said Ros, 'this baby was constantly protected, watched over and cared for in his mother's womb by the angels.'

Repent and be baptised, every one of you . . .

'. . . Every man needs to be born from above if he is going to see the kingdom of God. In listening to some presentations of the Gospel you get the impression that a man has to be a blackguard before Jesus Christ can do anything for him. It is true that Jesus Christ can make a saint out of any material, but the man down-and-out in sin is not the only class He deals with. It was to Nicodemus, a godly upright man, not to a sinner as we understand the term, that He said: "Marvel not that I said unto thee, Ye must be born again."

'What Jesus Christ does in new birth is to put in a disposition that transforms morality into holiness. He came to put into the man who knows he needs it. His heredity of holiness: to bring him into a oneness with God which he never had through natural birth. "That they may be one, even as We are one." '[1]

1 From Oswald Chambers: *Conformed to His Image* (Marshall, Morgan and Scott, London 1974)

How better than by these words of Oswald Chambers can I explain what I guess had prompted Shari mama to ask our fellowship leader to baptize her in water? Her decision came to us all as a surprise. She herself never gave us a detailed account of her motives – this would have been so much unlike her. She simply said: 'I want to obey Christ's command.' Those of us who knew her well were quite certain that she had not taken this decision lightly. Years of thought and prayer had ripened the desire: to bury all that was the 'old self' in order to be reborn, to be resurrected in Christ as a new creation. To be willing to act this out in baptism and publicly acknowledge the need for being renewed was a tremendous testimony from an eighty-three year old Jewish lady.

When Shari mama stood in the water, a frail and bent little figure in her white gown, with a net over her white hair, tears mingled with laughter while the fellowship gathered around her. It was an unforgettable occasion.

A time of grace

The St Luke Bath in Budapest and the attached hospital has long been established as a treatment centre for rheumatic and arthritic diseases. In the autumn of 1974 Shari mama decided to spend a fortnight there to get treatment to ease her aches and pains. Before starting the cure she wanted to stay for a week with a family living in Budapest who were dear and faithful friends.

We suspected all along that it was not the treatment she was after. This was only an excuse, even to herself, for going back once more to Hungary. Though her brother Pali had passed away since her last visit she was eager to meet her friends and relatives again, and refresh herself in their loving company.

On the planned date of her departure Valerie was due to give birth to their third child. It was Shari mama's hope that it would happen before she left and her desire was granted. On the very morning, just before we had to leave for the airport, Tommy rang with the good news of the arrival of another little girl to be named Karen. We drove jubilantly to the airport, singing on the way one of our beloved choruses: Sing Hosannah, sing Hosannah, sing Hossanah to the King of Kings . . .

I had several reports of the weeks she spent in Hungary from people who visited her in the hospital and who all wrote to us enthusiastically. Whoever went to see her praised her charming behaviour, her patient endurance of the often drastic treatment, her wit and humour and the fresh mind that was aware not only of what was happening closely around her but was equally well informed on world affairs. 'To converse with her is a pleasure,' wrote a friend, and apparently this was the opinion of others too because her hospital room was full of visitors every evening. Her room was like a garden with all the flowers she received.

The most moving letter came to us from Esther, her hostess for the week before she went to hospital. 'One day, after having knocked a few times on her door without an answer, I became concerned and carefully opened her door to avoid waking her in case she was asleep. I was frightened at first at what I saw. She was lying on the floor, on her face. But just then, not noticing me at all, she changed position, knelt at her bedside and seemed to be praying. Then again she went on her face. I stood there in complete amazement. Never have I seen anyone in such ardent and intensive prayer. I was embarrassed to have intruded on so intimate and sacred a moment and wanted to disappear silently, but then she noticed me. She got up from the floor and said in a very matter of fact manner that she was praying for Julie.'

This report came to me not at the time of Shari mama's stay there, but just recently, when Esther, having heard that I was planning to write about Shari mama's life, revealed this precious detail to me. It was so dear a memory to her, so secret an episode, that she had never mentioned it to anyone before. I was very moved when I received her letter.

I knew Shari mama prayed every morning for her loved ones all over the world, often raising her arms whilst sitting in bed (I sometimes intruded with her breakfast tray at such moments.) I also knew that she was greatly concerned for Julie. She made remarks like: 'This girl is missing her opportunities. She ought to come home, start a normal job, meet people and find the right man to marry.' That she was also praying towards this end was easy to guess. But that she was a real, fighting 'intercessor'–this she kept to herself. It was one of her sacred secrets.

The last chapter

After her return from Hungary in that autumn of 1974 Shari mama's heart started to function less well than before, water accumulated in her body and her tablets were incapable of checking the problem any more. For a while whenever she felt poorly, George prayed for her and she responded remarkably well. Then, one day in early May, Shari mama collapsed. Ros came and diagnosed that it was likely that a lot of water had accumulated in her chest thus causing the collapse. Shari mama spent a few weeks in bed, without getting up at all. She was very weak from her regular water-removing injections but she was quite comfortable and rested peacefully. Her features had smoothed out and she became very beautiful again. She enjoyed the company of friends who visited her and she was also reading a lot. The book she was reading just then was Eleanor Roosevelt's biography which interested her greatly and we discussed many of its political aspects together.

She apologized constantly for using me as a nurse as I washed her, emptied bedpans and so forth, although I reassured her that I did not mind this at all. In fact I found nursing her a satisfying and rewarding activity.

Her breathing gradually became noisier and one could hear the water moving in her chest. There were days when she was less alert and on some of those occasions she seemed to be hallucinating. She kept asking me whether I heard the music. There was nothing turned on! 'Do you hear them play?' she would ask. When I said that I did not, she sang to me what she had 'heard', mainly old songs, well known tunes. But on one occasion she asked: 'Do you hear what they sing?' and, conducting with both her arms, sang together with the unseen choir: Glory, Glory, Hallelujah . . .

When Ros came again I told her that Shari mama was repeatedly hearing music. She looked at me compassionately and said: 'The end may be very near. You must be prepared. Quite a few of my patients heard music a few days before they passed away.'

Ros, the dear faithful friend and doctor, now came sometimes more than once a day. She sometimes knelt next to the bedside and prayed with Shari mama. One day when she came three times, Shari mama was too weak to speak but shook her head, smiled, and lifted her hand indicating '3' with her fingers, acknowledging Ros's visits. Then, for a few days she picked up strength quite unexpectedly and was able to get up for short periods. She was very pleased with this achievement and planned to attend a meeting soon. One night her bell woke me. So far she had only used it during the day and I knew it was something very serious. I rushed to her room and found her in terrible pain. She who never used to complain, said that she could not bear the intensive pain in her chest. Ros was away for a couple of days just then and George hurried to call Dr M., whilst I sat there helplessly, seeing her suffering. This time the prayer did not help and Dr M. diagnosed an inner haemorrhage that had caused the heart to race, and also brought about the pain. He gave her injections for relief but before she fell asleep Shari mama indicated that she knew it was the end.

She slept for twelve hours. I sat next to her bed most of the time. Next evening, just after I had left her bedside for a little while, George called me to come up quickly: there was a change in her condition. When I rushed upstairs she had her eyes wide open. She seemed to be concentrating on something she saw, but she looked into the distance and took no notice of us. After a few minutes of silent gazing into a realm that was not ours she started to breathe heavily and a few seconds later passed away. It was all so silent, so peaceful. Graceful and dignified as her life, so was her death.

Family and friends were stunned. Despite her weak condition it had taken them by surprise. Many of them expressed how badly they would miss the sweet and positive personality that had been hers to the very end.

Her memorial service was a joyful thanksgiving rather than a funeral. Apart from the family, many friends from various backgrounds came. We chose to sing from Isaiah 35 verse 10: 'Therefore the redeemed of the Lord shall return . . .' and it was for us a joyful certainty that Shari mama would be among them. At the end of the service George read her favourite passage from 1 Corinthians 13. 'Love is patient and kind, it is not jealous or boastful, not arrogant or rude; love bears all things, believes all things, hopes all things and endures all things. Love never ends.' Here indeed, George pointed out, was someone who personified the kind of love the apostle described in that precious chapter.

In accordance with her wish she was cremated and the ashes placed at the roots of the rosebush originally to commemorate Dadi. The little board had to be changed to one with both their names on it. We ordered a text which we believed reflected the truth and was also an acknowledgement of her sanctified and sanctifying soul: 'Our Dadi and Shari mama unite and rejoice in God's Eternal Kingdom'.

Epilogue

Much has happened since my new year's resolution on 1 January 1982 to write Shari mama's biography.

1982 was a year of jubilee for our family. Twenty-five years had passed since we came to Britain. George and I celebrated our fortieth wedding anniversary in September and both our sons had their tenth anniversary during the year. Tommy, also, had his fortieth birthday. We tried to think of an appropriate way of expressing our joy and gratitude for God's grace with which we have been blessed over the past years. The solution which emerged was that we should spend a holiday, say a week, all together and during this time we should share with one another some of our cherished memories, our present interests and our hopes for the future.

As for the children – the fourth generation, Shari mama's great- grandchildren – time spent together would create its own happy memories as well as provide the enormous fun of such a family holiday. By now they made quite a crowd. 'Little' Andrew, Gillie, Danny, Mattie and Karen were the ones that Shari mama had known. Then there were those she had not lived to see: Hannah (also called Charlotte after her), who was born to John and Barbara after Shari mama's death, and Andrew and Peggie's daughter Louise, and their youngest, Georgie, born in October 1981, the only one to break the family pattern of blue eyes, looking out at the world through dark chocolate buttons. All eight are totally different in appearance and character – a delightful jumble of the various genes inherited and mixed in them.

We sought a suitable location for a gradually increasing

crowd (for some of the in-laws also wanted to take part in this venture). Eventually we decided on the boarding school of which Tommy had been headmaster for the last four years. It is in the West country, at a lovely spot surrounded by hills, fields and forests, and not far from the sea. During vacation time the buildings are unused and often let to organizations for holiday purposes. That year, therefore, we hired a block of comfortable size which was well equipped and ideal in every way for our venture. And there we had a tremendous holiday.

For my part, I think perhaps I enjoyed it even more than the others. I was able to observe the happy crowd and all its activities not only through my own but also through Shari mama's eyes. I sat on the patio in the sun, breathed in the fresh air, watched the sheep on the gentle slope opposite, white blobs on the lush green of the field, listened to the bleat of young lambs and reflected on the events that had occurred since Shari mama left us and imagined how she would have reacted to them. How happy and proud she would have been to know that Tommy, at the age of 35, has been appointed to the very responsible job of headmaster at this traditional old school. She would find it hard to believe that – like Tommy – John and Andrew are now approaching middle age, one an established college lecturer, the other an experienced architect and all three heads of their own growing families. How safely God has led and is continuing to lead us all!

You see, Shari mama, we too are growing old. I shall soon catch up with you with my wrinkles, bent fingers and almost grey hair.

Here my musing broke off as Hannah ran past, reminding me of yet another miracle. Before she was a year old her paediatrician had diagnosed a muscular failure and had cautiously told her parents that 'by the time she is five she might be walking' . . . What a sorrow it was for them and for all of us, yet John and Barbara, instead of despairing, took the diagnosis calmly, adjusted themselves to it but at the same time prayed for and believed in Hannah's healing. The family was once again united in prayer and Ros, still our doctor, shared the concern and the prayers for the little girl who had such limp arms and legs. More tests were carried out and Hannah had to be taken regularly to hospital, but soon there was a surprising and remarkable change in her condition. Within weeks, without medication or any other treatment, her muscles began to work and within a couple of months she was running. It was God who had changed the course of her illness. Now, two years old, it was hard to stop her clambering up the climbing frames in the playground.

Julie was sitting next to me on the patio, also following Hannah with her eyes. She rested her heavy body comfortably while doing a bit of sewing. 'I wonder what *our* baby will be like?' she asked herself. Hers was due soon and it had been just possible to take part in the joint holiday during the last weeks of her pregnancy. She and her husband Len joined us from Liverpool where they live.

Len had come on to the scene during the last few months of Shari mama's life but Julie's desire that Shari mama might still be with us and present at her wedding was not granted. How she would have enjoyed the day, when her prayers for Julie's happiness were finally answered!

Both Len and Julie spent years in Christian work; obediently carrying out often quite humble jobs as they were allocated to them, thus being prepared for the fulfilment of more responsible tasks. Len is now the leading elder of a big fellowship in Liverpool, the same one that Julie used to visit during her Manchester college years. Had someone suggested to her then that one day she would function there as an elder's wife she would hardly have believed it. By the time I write this epilogue they are the happy parents of a little girl, Natanya Joy. Naming her thus was Len's decision: Natanya is a Hebrew name and means 'The one given by God'. Indeed, she was given as an extra bonus to our jubilee year.

Apart from having fun together, our holiday provided an opportunity for long conversations which led us to appreciate our 'common grounds' even more, as well as to understand

and to come to respect those points of view over which some of us differed.

After the main evening meal, I would peep into the kitchen where our four young men – Tommy, John, Andrew and Len – were washing and drying the dishes. This was their allocated daily task. Attired in aprons and with kitchen cloths in hand, they would begin earnest discussions which carried on long after their domestic duties were finished, often lasting late into the night after the children had gone to bed. Many topics came under scrutiny but the one which recurred constantly was of the way they individually interpreted the ethical and doctrinal details of the Christian faith they all shared. The four of them, though so closely related to one another, each advocated different variations on the same theme, according to their own personalities.

I was reminded by this of Christ's prayer which he left as a testament for his disciples: 'Holy Father, keep them in thy name which thou hast given me, that they may be one even as we are one . . .'. I could not help asking myself whether such a vision of unity, prayed for so fervently by Jesus, would ever become a reality among His followers.

One night, when George and I retired to our room, leaving the younger generation to carry on with their conversation, I began speculating aloud: 'I wonder what Shari mama's reaction would have been had she taken part in today's discussion? Which of the attitudes that our young people represented would she have identified herself with?'

George, already in bed, looked at the clock and then, to my surprise, prepared himself, despite the late hour, to reflect on my hypothetical question. He began slowly, pensively: 'I think Shari mama would have listened to the conversation silently, without comment; she would not have taken sides but would have remained impartial even in her thoughts. Then, after a while, she would have taken her leave saying that it was time for her to go to bed and would have done so – just like I did tonight.'

Here he suppressed a little yawn and continued: 'Then, I

suppose, after turning off the light she would have sent up a simple prayer to the Heavenly Father for her loved ones. She would have prayed that the Holy Spirit should bring forth the unity that we human beings, even Christian believers, find so hard to achieve.'

With yet another yawn, no longer suppressed, George turned over and murmered: 'I guess that after this, Shari mama would have considered the issue closed as far as she was concerned and would have peacefully fallen asleep. So, my dear, what if you followed her example?'

Autumn 1984

Two years have gone by since I finished writing the story of Shari mama, concluding with the epilogue above. I gave duplicated copies to members of the family and some close friends, as was my original intention. Their positive comments encouraged me to polish up the manuscript with a view to publication. This is how this book has come into existence. However, before putting in my final full stop, I wish to acknowledge the work of the Holy Spirit in the young members of our family during these past two years.

First, one would notice a change at family gatherings when they shared their experiences. Discussions about theoretical and doctrinal issues have come up less frequently; instead, topics like God's guidance, and how best to obey it, have received the main emphasis not only in their conversation but also in the outward manifestations of their lives.

John, though well established in his teaching job in London, felt that he had to respond to an appeal for more Christian teachers in the schools run by the Africa Inland Mission. He and Barbara have applied, and been accepted, and the place appointed to them is a boarding school in Kenya where they will teach several subjects between them. Their children, Mattie and Hannah, will also be able to carry on their education there. They left in August for a spell of three years. We are going to miss them very much yet we believe that God will bless their venture and they will be able to do good work in Kenya.

Whilst Andrew's career as an architect has unfolded itself in a very promising way, at the same time many new members have joined the fellowship of which he is one of the elders. He feels that he has to choose one way or another: either to remain at his job with its ever increasing demands or to go full time into the ministry, in response to the needs of the growing church where the amount of work is becoming too much for the present full time leader. Andrew and Peggie are praying for guidance and a decision should follow shortly.

On the other hand, for Len and Julie the obvious course was to carry on in Liverpool – at the same place, in the same position, Len leading the church and its various enterprises: the foundation and enlargement of a private Christian school, the running of a bookshop with a cafeteria, etc.

Tommy also still heads the same boarding school. He has acquired valuable experience during the past years on how to bring up children and teenagers in a school which is basically liberal, demanding at the same time discipline both in behaviour and in study. To work out a healthy combination of the two seemingly contradictory approaches has been, I believe, Tommy's special task, to which Valerie has given faithful support.

Thus, each of the four young couples has discovered an important truth: when yielding to the guidance of the Holy Spirit – whether it is to 'stay' or to 'go' – God provides grace and power to function well at the appointed place.

Although their personal vocations might keep them geographically apart (one family in London, one in Kenya, one in Liverpool and one in the West Country), spiritually they have become very close through common experiences. It is a great joy for us to observe this oneness that has developed over and above their bond of love and friendship.

For the increasing spiritual unity in our small family, and among God's children in the worldwide family of believers, praise and glory be to our patient and wise Heavenly Father.